Paso por Paso

Dr. Susan Savage Lee

Kendall Hunt
publishing company

Contents

Capítulo Preliminar: Introduction

(Madrid, España)

0.1 Subject Pronouns

In Spanish, subject pronouns to refer to yourself and others. For example: I, you, he, she, they, and we. The following subject pronouns can be used to address groups or to address people in formal and informal ways.

yo	I
tú	you (informal)
él	he
ella	she
Ud. (usted)	you (formal)
nosotros/as	we
ellos	they (masculine or mixed group)
ellas	they (feminine)
Uds. (ustedes)	you (formal, plural)

Most of the subject pronouns listed above are used the same way that we use them in English. The only difference is that with **nosotros/as, ellos**, and **ellas,** you have to pay attention to the gender of the group. These subject pronouns are all plural, whereas **yo, tú, él, ella,** and **Uds**. are singular subject pronouns.

0.2 Gender and Number

If you are addressing a group of men, you use **ellos**. If you are addressing a mixed audience (both men and women), you use **ellos**. If you are addressing a group of women, you use **ellas**. **Nosotros** follows these same rules.

As you can see, all nouns in Spanish, including subject pronouns, are considered masculine or feminine. These nouns are either singular or plural. The common masculine ending of singular nouns is -**o.** The common feminine ending of singular nouns is -**a.** The common masculine ending for plural nouns is -**os.** The common feminine ending for plural nouns is -**as.**

Keep in mind that the gender of an object has nothing to do with contemporary understanding of masculinity or femininity.

Here are some examples of the gender and number of nouns in Spanish:

el chico	the young boy (masculine, singular)
la chica	the young girl (feminine, singular)
los chicos	the young boys (masculine, plural)
las chicas	the young girls (feminine, plural)

In Spanish, you always have to pay attention to the gender and number of nouns to make a sentence grammatically correct.

> **HINT:** There are some nouns and adjectives that do not follow the **-o** masculine ending and the **-a** feminine ending. For example:

la mano	the hand (feminine)
el mapa	the map (masculine)
el día	the day (masculine)
la foto	the photo (feminine)

0.3 Definite Articles

Definite articles are used to talk about any type of noun in Spanish. These articles are **el, la, los,** and **las.** The common translation of this in English is "the." As you can see, definite articles agree in gender and number with the nouns that they precede.

el	masculine, singular
la	feminine, singular
los	masculine, plural
las	feminine, plural

el libro	the book
los libros	the books
la casa	the house
las casas	the houses

0.4 The Verb Ser

© Catarina Belova/Shutterstock.com

A useful and very common verb in Spanish is **ser** (to be). Below you will find the forms of ser in the present tense.

yo	soy	I am
tú	eres	you are (informal)
él	es	he is
ella	es	she is
Ud.	es	you are (formal)
nosotros/as	somos	we are

ellos	son	they (all men or a mixed group) are
ellas	son	they (all women) are
Uds.	son	you are (formal, plural)

0.5 Uses of Ser

Ser is used to describe profession, identity, where someone is from (origin), nationality, physical characteristics, and telling time.

Ella es bonita.	She is pretty.
Nosotros somos italianos.	We are Italian.
Tú eres profesora.	You are a professor.
Él es estudiante.	He is a student.
Yo soy de Ecuador.	I am from Ecuador.
Es la una.	It is one o'clock.

> **HINT:** Because each verb form is different for each subject, you can drop your subject pronoun to avoid repetition when speaking or writing, like this:
>
> *Eres profesora.* You are a professor.
> *Soy de Ecuador.* I am from Ecuador.

Or you can keep them, like this:

Tú eres profesora.

Yo soy de Ecuador.

Ser is also used with specific questions associated with introducing oneself to others.

¿De dónde eres? Where are you from?

¿De dónde son? Where are they from?

0.6 Un Momento Cultural: Accent Marks

¿ á é í ó ú ñ

In Spanish, it is important to use accent marks like those listed above. An accent mark provides emphasis when speaking a specific letter. In English, we learn where to put the emphasis when speaking a word; however, we don't actually have a written accent mark above the letter or syllable. It is important to remember accent marks in Spanish because they can also change the meaning of a word. For example, **qué** (what) versus **que** (that, than). Getting used to accent marks early on will help you learn pronunciation and varied word meanings.

0.7 Conversación

Now that you've learned how to form basic sentences, you need to learn how to ask and answer introductory questions.

¿Cómo te llamas?	What is your name?
¿Cómo se llama?	What is his/her name?
Hola.	Hello
¿Qué tal?	How is it going? (informal)
Bien/mal.	Good/bad.
Buenos días.	Good morning
Buenas tardes.	Good afternoon.
Buenas noches.	Good evening.
Adiós.	Goodbye

Hasta pronto.	See you soon.
Hasta mañana.	See you tomorrow.
Chau. Nos vemos.	We'll be seeing each other.
Ciao.	Bye.

0.8 Telling Time in Spanish

Just like everything else in Spanish, telling time involves paying attention to the number of hours and their gender.

la hora	the hour
el día	the day
la mañana	the morning

la tarde	the afternoon
la noche	the night
el mediodía	noon
la medianoche	midnight
Es la una.	It is one o'clock.
Son las dos.	It is two o'clock.

In English, we use "it" to refer to the hour. In Spanish, we treat "hour" as feminine and singular, or feminine and plural. If it is one o'clock, we use the third-person singular version of ser (es). If it is more than one hour, we use the third-person plural of ser (son). For example:

Es la una.	It is one o'clock.
Son las tres.	It is three o'clock.
Son las cuatro.	It is four o'clock.
Son las cinco.	It is five o'clock.

If you want to describe fifteen minutes after an hour, you can use **quince** (fifteen) or **cuarto** (quarter).

Es la una y cuarto. Or: *Es la una y quince.* It is 1:15. It is a quarter past one.

Son las dos y quince. Or: *Son las dos y cuarto.* It is 2:15. It is a quarter past two.

If you want to describe half an hour past the hour, you can use **media** or **treinta** (thirty).

Es la una y media. Or: *Es la una y treinta.* It is half past one. It is 1:30.

Son las dos y treinta. Or: *Son las dos y media.* It is half past two. It is 2:30.

To describe a few minutes before the hour, subtract those minutes from the next hour. For example:

Son las dos menos diez. It is 1:50. (Literally: It is ten minutes before two).

Son las dos menos cuarto. It is 1:45. (Literally: It is a quarter till two).

Helpful phrases

¿A qué hora....?	At what time....?
¿Qué hora es?	What time is it?
de/por las mañanas	in the mornings
de/por las tardes	in the afternoons
de/por las noches	in the evenings

0.9 Vocabulario: Las Materias Escolares – Subjects of Study

© 976photo Studio/Shutterstock.com

Las lenguas extranjeras, los idiomas extranjeros (foreign languages)

el alemán	German
el chino	Chinese
el italiano	Italian
el español	Spanish
el inglés	English
el japonés	Japanese
el francés	French
el portugués	Portuguese

Las ciencias naturales (natural sciences)

la astronomía	astronomy
la biología	biology
la física	physics
la química	chemistry

Las humanidades (humanities)

el arte	art
la literatura	literature
la filosofía	philosophy
la religión	religion
el teatro	theater

Las ciencias sociales (social sciences)

la historia	history
la psicología	psychology
la antropología	anthropology
la economía	economics
la geografía	geography
las ciencias políticas	political science

HINT: When writing out languages or describing nationality, do not capitalize the first letter of the word in Spanish as you do in English. For example: inglés/English, francés/French.

0.10 Verbs Like Gustar and Indirect Object Pronouns

© Omnart/Shutterstock.com

In order to express likes and dislikes in Spanish, you will need to understand verbs like **gustar**. In contrast to verbs like ser, these verbs do not follow the same sentence structure. For example:

Ser: Yo soy estudiante. **Word order**: Subject/verb/object

Gustar: Me gusta la clase. **Word order**: Indirect object pronoun/verb/ subject

When working with verbs like gustar, what is first in the sentence is called the **indirect object pronoun** rather than the subject pronoun (yo, tú, ella, etc.). The following are indirect object pronouns and their meanings in Spanish:

me	to/for	me
te	to/for	you (informal)
le	to/for	him, her, or Ud.
nos	to/for	us
les	to/for	them or Uds.

The subject, in general, will appear *last* in the sentence. For example:

Me gusta la clase. The class is pleasing to me/ I like the class.

Me gustan las clases. The classes are pleasing to me/ I like the classes.

Nos gusta la clase. The class is pleasing to us/ We like the class.

Nos gustan las clases. The classes are pleasing to us/ We like the classes.

> **HINT:** If you need to clarify who the indirect object pronoun is referring to, then you use the **personal "a."** You use the personal "a" in front of each person's name or identity, even when there are multiple people. For example:
>
> *A Susana le gusta la clase.* The class is pleasing to Susana/ Susana likes the class.
> *A Raúl y a Pedro les gusta la clase.* The class is pleasing to Raúl and Pedro/ Raúl and Pedro like the class.

If you want to negate the action of a sentence in Spanish, including when using verbs like gustar, put "no" in front of the verb.

*A Susana **no** le gusta la clase.* The class is not pleasing to Susana. Susana does not like the class.

*A Raúl y a Pedro **no** les gusta la clase.* The class is not pleasing to Raúl and Pedro. Raúl and Pedro do not like the class.

> **HINT:** With verbs like gustar, other verbs can function as subjects of the sentence. For example:
>
> *Me gusta cantar y bailar.* Singing and dancing are pleasing to me/I like to sing and dance.

When this is the case, use the third–person singular form of the verb: gusta, fascina, interesa, etc.

Here is a list of verbs that follow the same word order (syntax) as gustar:

fascinar	to fascinate
faltar	to miss
molestar	to bother
encantar	to enchant
interesar	to interest

0.11 Vocabulario: La Característica Física – Physical Characteristics

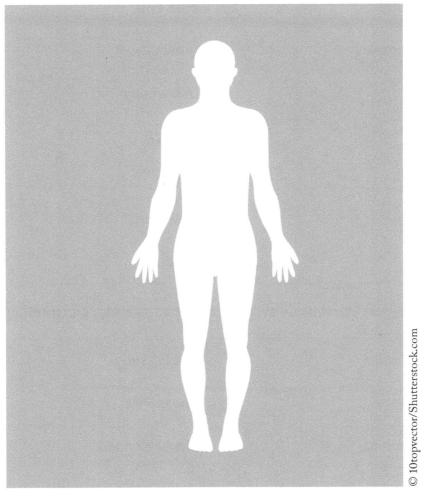

© 10topvector/Shutterstock.com

alto/alta	tall
bajo/a	short
delgado/a	thin, slender
gordo/a	fat
flaco/a	kinny
rubio/a	blonde
moreno/a	dark-haired
pelirrojo/a	red-haired
ojos verdes	green eyes
ojos azules	blue eyes
ojos marrones	brown eyes
viejo/a	old, elderly
joven	young
bonito/a	pretty
guapo/a	handsome
feo/a	Ugly

When using adjectives like this, always pay attention to **gender** and **number**. For example:

Ella es bonit**a**.	She is pretty.
Ella es baj**a**.	She is short.
Ella es rubi**a**.	She is blonde.

El hombre es bajo.	The man is short.
El hombre es alto.	The man is tall.
El hombre tiene ojos marrones.	The man has brown eyes.
La mujer tiene ojos verdes.	The woman has green eyes.
La mujer es vieja.	The woman is elderly.
El chico es joven.	The boy is young.

> **HINT:** Notice that the adjective appears *after the noun* like this: **ojos verdes**. In English, we put the adjective before the noun like this: green eyes.

0.12 Possessive Adjectives

mi	my (singular)	mis	my (plural)
tu	your (singular, informal)	tus	your (plural, informal)
su	his/hers/their (singular)	sus	his/her/ their (plural)
nuestro/a	our (singular)	nuestros/as	our (plural)

With most possessive adjectives, you just have to pay attention to number (singular vs. plural). In the case of **nuestro/a,** you have to pay attention to gender as well. For example:

Mis clases son interesantes. My classes are interesting.

Mi clase es interesante. My class is interesting.

Su novela es interesante. Her/his/your (formal) novel is interesting.

Sus novelas son interesantes. Her/his/their novels are interesting.

Nuestra clase es aburrida. Our class is boring.

Nuestro libro es aburrido. Our book is boring.

Nuestros libros son interesantes. Our books are interesting.

Nuestras ideas son interesantes. Our ideas are interesting.

> **HINT:** If you want to say the English equivalent of "a/an" before a noun, use "un/una." Like with everything else in Spanish, you must make it agree in gender and number. Un/una is referred to as an **indefinite article**. For example:

una amiga hermosa	a beautiful friend
unas amigas hermosas	beautiful friends
un mal chico	a bad boy
unos chicos malos	bad boys

0.13 Un Momento Cultural: El Flan

Like with any country, there are specific foods associated with Mexican culture. Flan, a Mexican desert (**el postre**), has its origins in Greek and Roman society. After the fall of these cultures, flan made its way to Spain. While the Romans used ingredients like eel in their version of flan, Spaniards made it a sweet dessert, using caramelized sugar to do so. With the arrival of the Spanish in the New World, flan made its way to what is now Mexico. From: https://mexicanfoodjournal.com/traditional-mexican-flan-napolitano/

© Natali Zakharova/Shutterstock.com

Flan
Ingredientes:

¼ cup of water (el agua)

1 and ½ cups of sugar (el azúcar)

3 cups of milk (la leche)

3 large egg yolks (las yemas de huevo)

1 teaspoon pure vanilla extract (el extracto de vainilla)

4 large eggs (los huevos)

Related vocabulary

el horno	oven
el cuchillo	knife
el bol	bowl
la cacerola	saucepan
revolver	to stir
hornear	to bake
verter	to pour
mezclar	to mix

0.14 Vocabulario: Descriptive adjectives

¿Te gustan tus clases? (Do you like your classes?)

interesante	interesting
bueno/a	good
malo/a	bad
aburrido/os	boring (masculine forms)
aburrida/as	boring (feminine forms)
divertido/os	fun (masculine forms)
divertida/as	fun (feminine forms)
regular	regular

Mis clases son interesantes y divertidas. My classes are interesting and fun.

Mi clase es interesante y divertida. My class is interesting and fun.

Mis libros son aburridos. My books are boring.

Mi libro es aburrido. My book is boring.

HINT: Descriptive adjectives have to agree in gender and number with what they are modifying. With bueno and malo, there is some flexibility in word order. When you switch the order of bueno or malo, the meaning is not altered. For example:

el profesor bueno	the good professor
el buen profesor	the good professor
el profesor mal	the bad professor
el mal profesor	the bad professor

0.15 Gramática: Numbers 1–30

© Design tech art/Shutterstock.com

uno	one
dos	two
tres	three
cuatro	four
cinco	five
seis	six
siete	seven
ocho	eight
nueve	nine
diez	ten
once	eleven
doce	twelve
trece	thirteen
catorce	fourteen
quince	fifteen
dieciséis	sixteen
diecisiete	seventeen
dieciocho	eighteen
diecinueve	nineteen
veinte	twenty

veintiuno	twenty-one
veintidós	twenty-two
veintitrés	twenty-three
veinticuatro	twenty-four
veinticinco	twenty-five
veintiséis	twenty-six
veintisiete	twenty-seven
veintiocho	twenty-eight
veintinueve	twenty-nine
treinta	thirty

The word **hay** (there is/there are) is often used with numbers. For example:

Hay tres chicos en la clase. There are three boys in the class.

Hay un chico en la familia. There is a boy in the family.

Hay dos jóvenes en el parque. There are two young people in the park.

Hay cuatro clases de literaturaen el departamento de inglés. There are four literature classes in the English department.

HINT: Notice that even question marker words like cuánto/os/a/as must agree with their subjects' gender and number:

¿**Cuántas chicas** hay en la clase?	How many girls are there in the class?
¿**Cuántos chicos** hay en la clase?	How many boys are there in the class?
¿**Cuántos libros** hay en la biblioteca?	How many books are there in the library?
¿**Cuántas revistas** hay en la librería?	How many magazines are there in the bookstore?

0.16 Un Momento Cultural: Facts About Mexico

© Magi Bagi/Shutterstock.com

Datos sobre México

1. El nombre oficial de México es los Estados Unidos Mexicanos.

2. La comida (food): El tamale se llama zacahuil.

3. La Universidad de México se fundió (was founded) en 1551 por Carlos V de España.

4. The size of México is 756,066 square miles.

5. Mexico is the fourteenth largest country in the world.

6. Mexico is located in the "Ring of Fire," one of the most violent volcano and earthquake zones.

7. In Spanish-speaking countries like Mexico, **mestizo** is used to describe someone with Indian-Spanish ethnicity.

8. Creoles are descendants of Spanish people who first arrived in Mexico.

9. Mexico introduced chocolate to the world (**el chocolate**).

10. In Spanish–speaking countries like Mexico, soccer is called **fútbol**. American football is called **fútbol americano**.

> **HINT:** In Spanish, both **tú** and **Ud.** mean "you." However, tú is used to informally address people, while Ud. is used to formally address people. Here is a list of circumstances that would require formality: speaking to your boss, someone with a high position such as a president of a country, doctors, lawyers, or teachers (depending on the formality of your relationship with them). Speaking to friends, family, acquaintances, or children would most likely require the tú form. In social situations, there is always some flexibility; however, it is always best to be more polite than to be rude when you are not sure what the social customs require for a certain situation.

0.17 Extra Vocabulary

© MinskDesign/Shutterstock.com

Mi nombre es _____.	My name is _____.
Mucho gusto.	Pleased to meet you.
¿Cómo se dice...?	How does one say ...?
No comprendo.	I don't understand
No entiendo.	I don't understand
No sé.	I don't know.
Otra vez, por favor.	Again, please.

Repita, por favor.	Repeat, please.
Tengo una pregunta.	I have a question
tengo	I have
tienes	you (informal) have
las comunicaciones	communications
la composición	writing
hablar en público	public speaking
otras materias	other subject
la especialización	major
la administración de empresas	business administration
la agricultura	agriculture
la agronomía	agriculture
el cálculo	calculus
la computación	computer science
la contabilidad	accounting
la educación física	physical education
la enfermería	nursing
la informática	computing
la ingeniería	engineering
la justicia criminal	criminal justice

el mercadeo or marketing	marketing
el periodismo	journalism
¿Qué carrera haces?	What is your major?
No lo sé todavía.	I don't know yet.
algunos	some (masculine)
algunas	some (feminine)
mucho	much (masculine, singular)
mucha	much (masculine, feminine)
muchos	many
muchas	many
poco	little
poca	little
pocos	few
pocas	few
el amigo	friend (male)
la amiga	friend (female)
el país	country
el examen	exam
gracias	thanks
muy	very

aquí	here
de	of; from
y	and

0.18 Study Tips

Learning another language can be intimidating, especially when it comes to remembering vocabulary. If you are having trouble remembering new vocabulary words, try the following tips:

1. Make flashcards (either on notecards or via free sites like Quizlet). Work with a small number of vocabulary words at a time (maybe ten to fifteen). Once you can remember these words easily, gradually add new ones. Be sure to review older vocabulary words once in a while to keep them fresh in your memory.

2. Use a group of vocabulary words in basic sentences, like this: **Yo tengo un gato**. I have a cat. **Yo quiero aprender español**. I want to learn Spanish. Using vocabulary words in everyday sentences will help you retain what you learn.

3. Practice reading vocabulary words out loud along with their translations if you learn best via auditory methods.

Capítulo 1
TIME

© Tata8848/Shutterstock.com

1.1 The Verb Estar – to be

In the Capítulo Preliminar, you learned about the verb **ser** (to be). There is also another verb in Spanish that means the same thing: **estar**. Like ser, estar is used in specific situations, namely present location and health/wellbeing. For example:

Estoy en casa. I am at home.

Ella está en la biblioteca. She is in the library.

¿Cómo estás? How are you?

Estoy enferma. I am sick.

Here are the different conjugations of estar in the present tense:

yo	estoy	I am
tú	estás	you (informal) are
él, ella, Ud.	está	he, she, you (formal) is/are
nosotros	estamos	we are
ellos, ellas, Uds.	están	they, you (formal) are

1.2 Un Momento Cultural: Apostrophes in Spanish

There are no apostrophes in Spanish to show ownership or possession. Instead, when you want to show possession like in "Mary's book," then you use the **"de"** construction. For example:

El libro de Mary. Mary's book.

El gato de la chica. The girl's cat.

El perro de la mujer. The woman's dog.

1.3 The Present Tense

In Spanish, there are three different types of verbs: **-ar ending, -er ending**, and **-ir ending**. To conjugate the verbs in the present tense, simply remove the endings and then add the respective new endings to each verb group. As in English, the present tense is used to describe the current moment.

Trabajar – to work

| yo | trabajo |
| tú | trabajas |

él, ella, Ud.	trabaja
nosotros/as	trabajamos
ellos, ellas, Uds.	trabajan

Comer – to eat

yo	como
tú	comes
él, ella, Ud.	come
nosotros/as	comemos
ellos, ellas, Uds.	comen

Escribir – to write

yo	escribo
tú	escribes
él, ella, Ud.	escribe
nosotros/as	escribimos
ellos, ellas, Uds.	escriben

Ellos escriben una carta. They write a letter.

Yo trabajo con Ricardo. I work with Ricardo.

Nosotros comemos una ensalada. We eat a salad.

HINT: In Spanish, two verbs cannot be conjugated if they are next to each other. The grammatical rule is to conjugate the first verb while leaving the second one in its infinitive state. This type of sentence structure is also found in English. For example:

Me gusta escribir. Writing is pleasing to me/ I like to write.
Yo aprendo escribir bien. I learn to write well.
Mi familia aprende hablar español. My family is learning how to speak Spanish.

1.4 Vocabulario: Regular Verbs in the Present Tense

© patpitchaya/Shutterstock.com

acabar	to complete, to finish
aceptar	to accept
afeitar	to shave
amar	to love
ayudar	to help, to assist
bailar	to dance
bañar	to bathe, to wash

besar	to kiss
cambiar	to change
caminar	to walk
cantar	to sing
cenar	to eat dinner/supper
comprar	to buy
cortar	to cut
cuidar	to guard
dejar	to leave
desayunar	eat breakfast
desear	to wish, desire
dibujar	to draw
disfrutar	to enjoy
disgustar	to disgust
duchar	to shower
dudar	to doubt
enojar	to anger
enseñar	to show, to teach
entrar	to enter
escuchar	to listen, to hear

estudiar	to study
fumar	to smoke
ganar	to win
gastar	to spend
gritar	to scream, to shout, to yell
hablar	to speak, to talk
lastimar	to injure, to hurt
lavar	to wash
limpiar	to clean
llamar	to call
llevar	to take, to wear
llorar	to cry
mandar	to send, to command
manejar	to drive
mirar	to watch, to see, to look
molestar	to annoy, to bother
nadar	to swim
necesitar	to need
ocupar	to occupy
olvidar	to forget

participar	to participate
pasar	to pass time, to spend time
pintar	to paint
planchar	to iron
preguntar	to ask a question
prepaar	to prepare
presta	to lend, to borrow
terminar	to terminate, to end
tomar	to drink, to take
trabajar	to work
usar	to use
viajar	to travel
visitar	to visit
voltear	to turn
vomitar	to vomit

HINT: When asking a question in Spanish, be sure to put the subject *after* the verb. The word order changes when asking a question.

¿Tomas tú el sol?
¿Practica Ud. el violín?
¿Escuchan Uds. la música country?

1.5 Vocabulario: Days of the Week

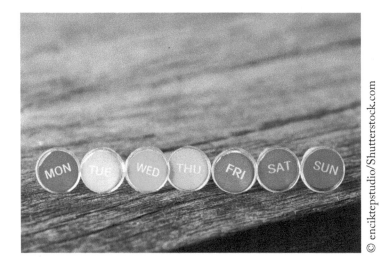

© enciktepstudio/Shutterstock.com

el lunes	Monday
el martes	Tuesday
el miércoles	Wednesday
el jueves	Thursday
el viernes	Friday
el sábado	Saturday
el domingo	Sunday

Elena practica deportes los lunes. Elena practices sports on Mondays.

El profesor cocina cada domingo. The professor cooks each Sunday.

Yo toco la guitarra los jueves. I play guitar on Thursdays.

1.6 Vocabulario: Months of the Year

© Bonitas/Shutterstock.com

el enero	January
el febrero	February
el marzo	March
el abril	April
el mayo	May
el junio	June
el julio	July
el agosto	August
el septiembre	September

el octubre	October
el noviembre	November
el diciembre	December

1.7 Vocabulario: Seasons of the Year

© Mihai_Andritoiu/Shutterstock.com

la primavera	spring
el verano	summer
el otoño	fall
el invierno	winter

1.8 Un Momento Cultural: Seasons in Argentina

ARGENTINA

INDEPENDENCE DAY

© chekart/Shutterstock.com

When it is winter in the United States, it is summer in Spanish-speaking countries like Argentina. This is because Argentina is part of the southern hemisphere. Conversely, when it is summer in the United States, it is winter in Argentina. While countries like Spain, more or less, mirror the seasons of the United States, our southern neighbors, like Argentina and Chile, do not.

1.9 Saber Versus Conocer

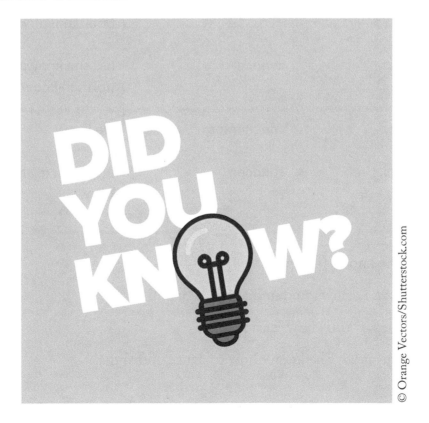

© Orange Vectors/Shutterstock.com

In Spanish, **saber** and **conocer** both mean "to know." However, much like ser and estar, they are used in different contexts. **Conocer** is used to talk about knowing or being familiar with people and places, while **saber** is used for knowing facts or pieces of information about something/someone, or how to do something. When conjugated in the present tense, saber and conocer have irregular forms in the yo form.

yo	sé	I know
tú	sabes	you (informal) know
él, ella, Ud.	sabe	he, she knows, you (formal) know
nosotros	sabemos	we know
ellos, ellas, Uds.	saben	they, you (formal) know
yo	conozco	I know (am familiar with)
tú	conoces	you (informal) know (are familiar with)
él, ella, Ud.	conoce	he, she knows, you (formal) know
nosotros	conocemos	we know
ellos, ellas, Uds.	conocen	they, you (formal) know

Conoce Cuba. She knows (is familiar with) Cuba.

Yo conozco España. I know (am familiar with) Spain.

Tú conoces a Enrique. You know Enrique.

Ella sabe bailar y cantar. She knows how to dance and sing.

Nosotros sabemos leer. We know how to read.

Yo sé el número de teléfono de Esteban. I know Esteban's phone number.

> **HINT:** When using **conocer** with people, you must use the personal "a." You do not need to use the personal "a" with places.

1.10 Stem-Changing Verbs in the Present Tense

© OneSideProFoto/Shutterstock.com

In Spanish, there are verbs that require you to change the stem before you add the proper -ar, -er, or -ir endings. These verbs are called **irregular verbs**. There are specific types of stem-changing verbs: **e-i**, **o-ue**, and **e-ie**.

Pedir – to ask for, to request (ei)

yo	pido
tú	pides
ella, él, Ud.	pide
nosotros	pedimos
ellos, ellas, Uds.	piden

Tener – to have (e-ie)

yo	tengo
tú	tienes
ella, él, Ud.	tiene
nosotros	tenemos
ellos, ellas, Uds.	tienen

Dormir – to sleep (o-ue)

yo	duermo
tú	duermes
ella, él, Ud.	duerme
nosotros	dormimos
ellos, ellas, Uds.	duermen

There is a fourth type of stem-changing verb, but it only affects jugar. For example:

Jugar – to play (u-ue)

yo	juego
tú	juegas
ella, él, Ud.	juega
nosotros/as	jugamos
ellos, ellas, Uds.`	juegan

> **HINT:** The stem-changing rule *does not* apply to nosotros/nosotras.

Common stem-changing verbs

empezar	to begin
repetir	to repeat
poder	to be able to
querer	to want
pensar	to think
perder	to lose
preferir	to prefer
soler	to tend to do something; to do something habitually
volver	to return
mover	to move (the body)
costar	to cost
seguir	to follow
decir	to say
sonreír	to smile

> **HINT:** When a verb is short, such as **seguir**, it is obvious which vowel to change because there is only one "e." However, with a longer verb like **preferir**, you should change the second vowel, in this case the second "e."

1.11 Un Momento Cultural: Chile

One of the traditional forms of dance in Chile is the **cusca**. Depending on the region where the dance is practiced (northern, southern, or central), cusca may be performed in different ways. Traditionally speaking, cusca is a blend of Spanish and indigenous cultural traditions. Cusca requires a partner. In fact, its origins stem from reenacting the courting ritual of the rooster and the hen. While the male partner dances with flamboyant ges-

tures, the female partner feigns coyness and shyness. The accompanying music usually involves the guitar (**la guitarra**) and the tambourine (**la pandereta**). The clothing worn during the dance ranges from all black to floral printed dresses (for women) and traditional ponchos and hats for men. Although the dancers never touch, the cusca involves dramatic gestures, usually expressed through facial expressions and eye contact. During the nineteenth century, the cusca could be found in bars and taverns. In more contemporary times, the cusca has been associated with national holidays and tournaments. In addition, contemporary cusca dancers have abandoned more traditional elements of the dance by varying the dance's velocity as well as the costumes. Cusca can also be found in parts of Argentina and Bolivia.

1.12 Study Tips

HINT: To address people formally, you can use Señora (Mrs.) or Señor (Mr.). When speaking to a married couple with the same last name, you use the following: los Simpsons.

Many times when learning a foreign language, students are encouraged to memorize vocabulary words, especially nouns. While this is definitely important (as the last chapter's study tips convey), at the same time it is also important to remember verbs. Without a verb, you cannot form a complete sentence. Here are some tips to help you remember stem changing verbs.

1. Pick three verbs that you have trouble remembering because of their irregular forms. Write them out in the present tense over and over again, until you can do so without hesitation.

2. While it is easy to identify stem changing verbs like **o-ue** ones, it is difficult to tell the difference between **e-i** and **e-ie** verbs. Make a list of each kind as you come across them. Over time, you will begin to associate the proper stem changes with each verb group.

Capítulo 2
EVERYDAY LIFE

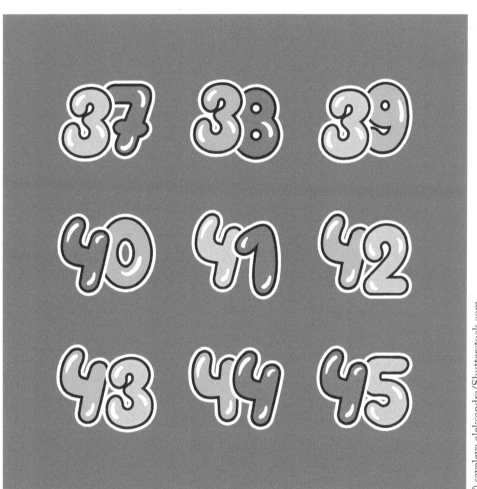

2.1 Numbers 31 and Higher

You have already learned numbers 0-30. Now you're going to learn numbers 30 and higher. They are:

treinta	30
cuarenta	40
cincuenta	50
sesenta	60
setenta	70
ochenta	80
noventa	90
cien, ciento	100

HINT: Use cien when you are trying to say 100. If you are trying to describe numbers beyond that, such as 115, then use ciento. For example: ciento quince (115) or ciento ocho (108).

Numbers higher than 100:

doscientos	200
trescientos	300
cuatrocientos	400
quinientos	500
seiscientos	600
setecientos	700

ochocientos	800
novecientos	900
mil	1,000
un millón/ millones	1,000,000

Notice that the "y" is only used when describing numbers below 100. For groups of hundreds, the "y" is not needed. For example:

ciento ochenta y siete   187

Here are a few examples to show you how to express larger numbers:

diecisiete mil seiscientos   17,600

cuatrocientos mil   400,000

> **HINT:** When writing Spanish numbers, Spanish-speaking cultures do not use the comma. Rather, they use a decimal point. For example: 265.000 instead of 265,000.

2.2 Reflexive Verbs

© VectorMine/Shutterstock.com

In Spanish, reflexive verbs are often used to express hygiene-oriented actions like bathing and showering. Reflexive verbs are also used to express some aspects of a daily routine. In English, we use reflexives sparingly, but in Spanish, reflexive verbs are utilized quite often. The easiest way to identify a reflexive verb is to look for the **-se ending**, such as lavarse.

To conjugate reflexive verbs, follow this rule:

Lavarse – to wash oneself

me lavo	I wash myself
te lavas	you wash yourself
se lava	he/she/you (formal) wash himself/ herself/yourself
nos lavamos	we wash ourselves
se lavan	they wash themselves

HINT: The **me, te, se,** and **nos** is not optional when conjugating these verbs. They must appear before the stem conjugation.

Common reflexive verbs

bañarse	to bathe oneself
maquillarse	to put make-up on oneself
acostarse	to put oneself to bed
afeitarse	to shave oneself
apurarse	to hurry up
arrodillarse	to kneel down
darse vuelta	to turn around

despertarse	to wake up
ducharse	to take a shower
levantarse	to get up
quedarse	to stay put
reirse	to laugh
secarse	to dry oneself off
sentarse	to sit oneself down
sentirse	to feel

> **HINT:** Sometimes, a verb does not require the reflexive aspect if the action is directed elsewhere. Reflexive verbs answer the question: who is the recipient of this action? For example:
>
> *Me lavo.* I wash myself.
> *Yo lavo el coche.* I wash the car.

2.3 Possessive Adjectives

© vectopicta/Shutterstock.com

Possessive adjectives sit in front of a noun to show who owns it. For example: **my book**, or **his car**. In Spanish, possessive adjectives work the same way. The only difference is that when you use possessive adjectives, you have to make sure that everything agrees in **number** and **gender**. While most of the possessive adjectives just require acknowledgement of number (singular versus plural) the **nuestro/a/as/os** forms also require gender.

Singular possessive adjectives

mi	my
tu	your (informal)
su	his, hers, your (formal)
nuestro/a	our

Plural possessive adjectives

nuestros/as	our
sus	their
mi amiga	my friend
tu amiga	your friend
su amiga	his/her, your (formal) friend
nuestra amiga	our friend

Mi libro es muy interesante. My book is very interesting.

Mis libros son interesantes. My books are interesting.

Nuestro hijo es muy inteligente. Our son is very intelligent.

Nuestros hijos son muy inteligentes. Our sons are very intelligent.

> **HINT:** Notice that **tú** with an accent over the "u" means **you**, the subject pronoun, while **tu** without an accent means **your**.
>
> **HINT:** When you need to provide clarification of who the "su" or "sus" is, you can use the "de" construction. For example:
>
> *Marco conoce a sus primos.* Marco knows her cousins.

To identify that it is "her cousins" instead of "his" or "your," you can say: *Marco conoce a los primos de ella.*

2.4 Vocabulario: La Familia — The Family

© Evgeny Atamanenko/Shutterstock.com

la tía	aunt
el hermano	brother
el cuñado	brother-in-law
el primo	cousin
la hija	daughter
la nuera	daughter-in-law

divorciado	divorced
el padre	father
el suegro	father-in-law
el nieto	grandchild
la nieta	granddaughter
el abuelo	grandfather
la abuela	grandmother
el marido	husband
casado	married
la madre	mother
la suegra	mother-in-law
el sobrino	nephew
la sobrina	niece
(el) huérfano	orphan
los padres	parents
la hermana	sister
la cuñada	sister-in-law

el hijo	son
el yerno	son-in-law

el hijastro	stepchild
el padrastro	stepfather
la madrastra	stepmother
el tío	uncle
la viuda	widow
el viudo	widower
la mujer	wife

HINT: In English, using double negatives is grammatically incorrect. In Spanish, however, double negatives are acceptable. For example:

No tengo *ni* hermanos *ni* hermanas. I do not have brothers or sisters.
Mi hermana **no** *es inteligente* **ni** *simpática.* My sister is not intelligent or ambitious.

2.5 Vocabulario: Weather

© IgorZh/Shutterstock.com

la lluvia	rain
la llovizna	drizzle
la nieve	snow
el viento	wind

la nubosidad	cloudy weather
la tormenta	storm
el trueno	thunder
el relámpago	lightening
la helada	frost
la niebla	mist
los claros	bright spells
el hielo	ice
el pronóstico	forecast
la tempestad	storm
el interior	interior
la costa	coast
los grados	degrees
centígrado	centigrade
la temperatura	temperature
el clima	climate
hace calor	it is hot
hace frío	it is cold
hace sol	it is sunny
hace viento	it is windy

hace fresco	it is cool
hay niebla	it is foggy
tengo calor	I am hot
hace buen tiempo	it is good weather
el sol	sun
el fuego	fire

HINT: When describing the weather, use the verb "**hacer**" which means **to do** or **to make**. For example:

hace calor (it is hot), or *hace frío* (it is cold).

2.6 Un Momento Cultural: Gauchos in Argentina

When you think of cowboys riding on the frontier, you may think of the United States. However, Argentina has its own version of the cowboy: the **gaucho.** Just like the American cowboy, the gaucho is associated with the frontier (referred to as the pampas in Argentina). In contrast to the cowboy, however, the gaucho wears loose-fitting pants. The gaucho uses a saddle made from a blanket and he carries a knife instead of a pistol. The gaucho is also known for carrying a **bola,** a leather-pronged instrument used to entangle an animal's legs. Just like the cowboy, the gaucho is a figure that is oftentimes used to describe Argentine national identity.

2.7 Tener and Venir

© Ekahardiwito/Shutterstock.com

Tener and **venir** are two common but irregular verbs in Spanish. They have unusual stem changes as you can see below:

Tener – to have

yo	tengo
tú	tienes
ella, él, Ud.	tiene
nosotros/as	tenemos
ellos, ellas, Uds.	tienen

Venir – to come

yo	vengo
tú	vienes
ella, él, Ud.	viene
nosotros/as	venimos
ellos, ellas, Uds.	vienen

2.8 Vocabulario: Expressions Using Tener

© Rawpixel.com/Shutterstock.com

In English we typically use "to be" to express age, hunger, thirst, etc. For example, I am thirsty or I am fifteen years old. In Spanish, **tener** is used in place of "to be" to describe age, thirst, hunger, and other important expressions.

tener _ años	to be _ years old
tener calor	to be hot
tener frío	to be cold

tener hambre	to be hungry
tener sed	to be thirsty
tener sueño	to be sleepy
tener miedo	to be frightened
tener prisa	to be in a hurry
tener razón	to be right
no tener razón	to be wrong
tener orgullo	to be proud
tener suerte	to be lucky

2.9 The Verb Ir + A

© Foxys Graphic/Shutterstock.com

The verb **ir** means **to go**. It automatically comes with the preposition "a" attached to it so that it means "to go to." Ir is an irregular verb with stem changes. To conjugate **ir**, follow the following model:

yo	voy
tú	vas

ella, él, Ud.	va
nosotros/as	vamos
ellos, ellas, Uds.	van

Here are some examples of ir:

Ellos van a la universidad. They go to the university.

Mis hermanos van a la biblioteca. My brothers go to the library.

Yo voy al supermercado. I go to the supermarket.

Tú vas a Buenos Aires. You go to Buenos Aires.

> **HINT:** To create adverbs (words in English with the -ly ending), just add **-mente** to the end of an adjective or noun. For example:
>
> final + mente = finalmente (finally)
> rápida + mente = rápidamente (rapidly)
> total + mente = totalmente (totally)

Here are some of the uses of adverbs:

Finalmente, yo voy a la universidad. Finally, I am going to the university.

Actualmente, no me gusta la clase. Actually, I do not like the class.

2.10 More with Ir + A

© atk work/Shutterstock.com

In the present tense, **ir** can have future tense connotations when paired with another verb. **Ir** + **a** can be used to describe what you are going to do at some point in the immediate future. For example:

Voy **a caminar** por el parque mañana. *I am going to walk through the park tomorrow.*

*Tú **vas a estudiar** mañana.* You are going to study tomorrow.

Compare the sentences above with the following sentences written in the present tense.

Camino por el parque. You walk in the park.

Tú estudias. You study.

HINT: It is important to note that ir + a is **not** the future tense. It simply has future tense connotations to it.

2.11 Acabar de

© Stig Kristensen/Shutterstock.com

Using two verbs together to create an expression

In Spanish, when using **acabar de**, it means: "to just have done something (in the very recent past)." Much like **ir +a** can have future tense connotations, **acabar de** can have past tense connotations. To conjugate **acabar de**, follow the rules of regular -ar ending verbs below:

yo acabo de (verb infinitive)	I just. . .
tú acabas de (verb infinitive)	you (informal) just. . .
él, ella, Ud. acaba de (verb infinitive)	he, she, you (formal) just
nosotros/as acabamos de (verb infinitive)	we just. . .
ellos, ellas, Uds. acaban de (verb infinitive)	they just. . .

Examples:

Acabo de terminar la tarea. I just finished the homework.

Elisa acaba de salir con su amiga. Elisa just went out with her friend.

Ellas acaban de nadar en la piscina. They just swam in the pool.

2.12 Volver A

© Dmitry Demidovich/Shutterstock.com

Volver a is another expression like **acabar de**. It means to do something again. Like **acabar de**, it is followed by a verb in its infinitive state. In contrast to acabar de, volver a can be formed using the present tense.

vuelvo a (verb infinitive)	yo vuelvo a
vuelves a (verb infinitive)	tú vuelves a
vuelve a (verb infinitive)	él, ella, Ud. vuelve a
volvemos a (verb infinitive)	nosotros volvemos a
vuelven a (verb infinitive)	ellos, ellas, Uds. vuelven a

Vuelvo a leer la carta. I read the letter again.

Jorge y Raúl vuelven a escribir el párrafo. Jorge and Raúl write the paragraph again.

2.13 Vocabulario: Colors

© KRIACHKO OLEKSII/Shutterstock.com

amarillo	yellow
anaranjado	orange
azul	blue
blanco	white
gris	gray
marrón	brown

morado	purple
negro	black
rojo	red
rosa	pink
verde	green

Words commonly associated with colors

el árbol	tree
la flor	flower
el cactus	cactus
el arbusto	bush
la enredadera	vine
la hoja	leaf
el tulipán	tulip
el tallo	stem
la margarita	daisy
el bulbo	bulb
la orquídea	orchid
la violeta	violet
la rosa	rose
el botón	bud

Examples:

Me gustan las flores rojas. I like red flowers.

La casa es azul y amarilla. The house is blue and yellow.

Los zapatos son azules y blancos. The shoes are blue and white.

> **HINT:** Notice that when working with colors, you have to make them agree in gender and number with the noun they are describing.

2.14 Un Momento Cultural: Paraguay

© Negro Elkha/Shutterstock.com

The government of Paraguay is structured much like it is in the United States. Paraguay is a democratic republic that is broken into three branches: executive, legislative, and judiciary. As in the United States, the executive branch is controlled by the president, while the legislative branch is maintained by the national Congress. The judiciary branch is divided into the Supreme Court, tribunals, and civil law courts.

In contrast to the United States, Paraguay has more than a bipartisan system, meaning that there are more than two dominant political parties. Some of the political parties in Paraguay are Patriotic Alliance for Change, Workers' Party, Paraguayan Humanist Party, and National Union of Ethical Citizens, to name a few.

2.15 Study Tips

© fizkes/Shutterstock.com

Practicing Listening Comprehension

The best way to develop your ear in Spanish is to listen to something that interests you. Maybe you like a Spanish-speaking musical artist. Maybe you like listening to audiobooks. Whatever it is that you like to listen to, listening to it in Spanish will help develop your ear for the language. But don't expect to understand every single word the first time. Keep in mind that you don't always understand every single word in your native language. So be patient with your abilities as you develop listening comprehension skills in Spanish. Try to pick out as many words as you can when you first listen to a song or a poem read aloud. Then, through repetition, try to hear more and more individual words or phrases. If you keep practicing, you will be able to understand more and more each time.

Capítulo 3
THE HOME

© Photographee.eu/Shutterstock.com

3.1 The Past Tenses: The Preterite Versus the Imperfect

In English, the basic past tense refers to actions viewed as being completed or a part of the past. For example: "I ate a cheeseburger" or "I went to the store." In Spanish, however, there are two basic past tenses. Like with **conocer vs. saber** or **ser vs. estar**, each tense is used for specific

© Denis Andricic/Shutterstock.com

circumstances. The **preterite tense** is used to describe events that are viewed as being completed. In addition to this, the preterite tense is generally characterized by specific time markers such as the hour of the day, a certain year, or other keywords. For example:

anoche	last night
anteayer	the day before yesterday
desde el primer momento	from the first time
durante dos siglos	for two centuries
el otro día	the other day
en ese momento	in this moment
entonces	then
esta mañana	this morning
esta tarde	this afternoon
el año pasado	last year
ayer	yesterday
la semana pasada	last week
el mes pasado	last month
hace dos días, años	two days ago, two years ago
ayer por la mañana	yesterday morning
ayer por la tarde	yesterday afternoon

To conjugate verbs in the preterite tense, follow these rules:

Hablar – to speak (-ar ending verbs)

yo	hablé	I spoke
tú	hablaste	you spoke
él, ella, Ud.	habló	he, she, you (formal) spoke
nosotros	hablamos	we spoke
ellos, ellas, Uds.	hablaron	you (formal, plural), they spoke

Comer – to eat (-er ending verbs)

yo	comí	I ate
tú	comiste	you ate
él, ella, Ud.	comió	he, she, you (formal) ate
nosotros	comimos	we ate
ellos, ellas, Uds.	comieron	you (formal, plural), they ate

Vivir – to live (-ir ending verbs)

yo	viví	I lived
tú	viviste	you lived
él, ella, Ud.	vivió	he, she, you (formal) lived
nosotros	vivimos	we lived
ellos, ellas, Uds.	vivieron	you (formal, plural), they lived

In contrast to the preterite tense, the **imperfect,** the other basic past tense, is used to talk about habitual or generalized actions from the past, what someone was doing when they were interrupted by something else, dates, age, descriptions of emotions, characteristics, or feelings. Keywords frequently associated with the imperfect are:

a menudo	often
a veces	sometimes
cada día	every day
cada semana	every week
cada mes	every month
cada año	every year
con frecuencia	frequently
de vez en cuando	from time to time
en aquella época	at that time
frecuentemente	frequently
generalmente	usually
muchas veces	many times
mucho	a lot
nunca	never
por un rato	for a while
siempre	always
tantas veces	many times

todas las semanas	every week
todos los días	all days
todo el tiempo	all the times
varias veces	several times

Follow these rules to conjugate verbs in the imperfect tense:

Hablar – to speak (-ar ending)

yo	hablaba	I spoke
tú	hablabas	you spoke
él, ella, Ud.	hablaba	he, she, you (formal) spoke
nosotros	hablábamos	we spoke
ellos, ellas, Uds.	hablaban	you (formal, plural), they spoke

Comer – to eat (-er ending verbs)

yo	comía	I ate
tú	comías	You ate
él, ella, Ud.	comía	He, she, you (formal) ate
nosotros	comíamos	We ate
ellos, ellas, Uds.	comían	They, you (formal, plural) ate

Vivir (-ir ending verbs)

yo	vivía	I lived
tú	vivías	You lived
él, ella, Ud.	vivía	he, she, you (formal) lived
nosotros	vivíamos	we lived
ellos, ellas, Uds.	vivían	they, you (formal, plural) lived

Preterite Examples

Anoche, yo leí muchos libros. Last night, I read many books.

En 1861, la guerra civil empezó en los Estados Unidos. In 1861, the Civil War began in the United States.

Ayer, hablé con mi profesora. Yesterday, I spoke with my professor.

Hace dos años, tú visitaste Argentina. Two years ago, you visited Argentina.

Ayer, me lavé, me maquillé, y caminé a la escuela. Yesterday, I washed, put on make-up, and walked to school.

Imperfect Examples

Todos los domingos, nosotros caminábamos por el parque. Every Sunday, we used to walk through the park.

Mi madre cocinaba cuando sonó el teléfono. My mother was cooking when the phone rang.

Era el 10 de junio. It was the tenth of June.

Yo tenía quince años cuando me gradué de la escuela secundaria. I was fifteen years old when I graduated from high school.

Me sentía enferma durante la cena. I felt sick during dinner.

Hacía frío esa noche. It was cold that night.

3.2 Irregular Verbs in the Preterite

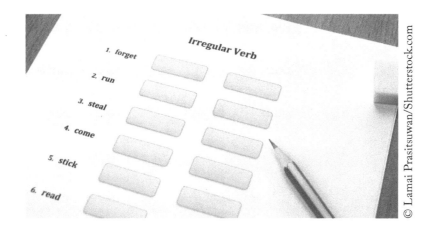

As with the present tense, there are irregular verbs in the preterite in Spanish. For example:

Tener

yo	tuve
tú	tuviste
él, ella, Ud.	tuvo
nosotros	tuvimos
ellos, ellas, Uds.	tuvieron

> **HINT:** Notice that irregular verbs in the preterite tense often do not have accent marks.

Common irregular verbs in the preterite tense with their stem changes

andar	anduv-	to walk
conducir	conduj-	to drive
decir	dij-	to say, to tell

estar	estuv-	to become
hacer	hic- and hiz-	to do, to make
poner	pus-	to put, place
*poder	pud-	to manage
*querer	quis-	to try
*no querer		to refuse
*saber	sup-	to find out
*tener	tuv-	to receive
venir	vin-	to come
ver	vi-	to see
dar	di-	to give
ir	fui, fuiste, fue, fuimos, fueron	to go
traer	traj-	to bring
ser	fui, fuiste, fue, fuimos, fueron to be	
*conocer	conoc-	to meet (not irregular, but has a different meaning)

Notice that **ser** and **ir** are conjugated the same way in the preterite tense. When using them, determine which verb is being used based on the context.

HINT: The verbs above with asterisks next to them change meaning in the preterite tense. For example:

Yo tengo una casa. I have a house. (Present tense)

Yo tuve una casa en octubre. I received a house in October. (Preterite)

Yo sé el número de teléfono de Stanley. I know Stanley's telephone number. (Present tense)

Yo supe la respuesta durante el exam. I found out the answer during the exam. (Preterite)

3.3 Irregular Verbs in the Imperfect

In contrast to the preterite tense, there are only three irregular verbs in the imperfect tense: **ver, ir, ser**. They are conjugated below:

Ver	
veía	yo veía
veías	tú veías
veía	él, ella, Ud. veía
veíamos	nosotros veíamos

veían	ellos, ellas, Uds. veían
Ir	
iba	yo iba
ibas	tú ibas
iba	él, ella, Ud. iba
ibamos	nosotros íbamos
iban	ellos, ellas, Uds. iban
Ser	
era	yo era
eras	tú eras
era	él, ella, Ud era
éramos	nosotros éramos
eran	ellos, ellas, Uds eran

Irregular and regular verbs in the imperfect do not change meaning.

3.4 Comparisons of Inequality

In Spanish, it is sometimes necessary to compare two things that may or may not be similar. When they differ, these comparisons are called comparisons of inequality. Comparisons of inequality involve suggesting that one thing is better than another. Comparisons of inequality follow a specific formula:

Más (more) + adjective + que

Menos (less) + adjective + que

más/menos + noun + que

más/menos + adverb + que

*Yo soy **más alta que** tú*. I am **taller than** you.

*Tú tienes **menos clases que** yo*. You have **fewer classes than** I.

*Gisela corre **más lentamente que** yo*. Gisela runs **more slowly than** I.

> HINT: Ina negative sentence, **que** combined with numbers means "only."

*No tienes más **que diez** dólares*. You only have ten dollars.

If a number follows in the comparison, que becomes "de."

*Yo tengo más **de cinco** naranjas.* I have **more than five** oranges.

*Hay menos **de diez** estudiantes en la clase de ciencias políticas.* There are **less than ten** students in the political science class.

3.5 Vocabulario: The Home

© Breadmaker/Shutterstock.com

la casa	house
el apartamento	apartment
la cocina	the kitchen
el comedor	dining room
la sala de estar/el salón	living room
el baño	bathroom
la habitación	bedroom
el cuarto de invitados	guest bedroom

3.6 Comparisons of Equality

Comparisons of equality are used to compare similarities or things that you judge to be equal. They work using a similar formula as comparisons of inequality:

Tan + adjective (or adverb) como

*Soy **tan alta como** mi hermana.* I am **as tall as** my sister.

*Ella corre **tan rápidamente como** su hermano.* She runs **as quickly as** her brother.

When making comparisons of equality with nouns, make whichever version of **tanto** used agree in gender and number with the noun.

*Tengo **tantos libros** como tú.* I have **as many books** as you.

*Mi madre tiene **tantas clases** como yo.* My mother has **as many classes** as I.

tantos/as/o/a + noun + como

3.7 Vocabulario: The Bathroom

la bañera	bathtub
el inodoro, el aseo	toilet
el lavabo	sink
el botiquín, el gabinete de la medicina	medicine cabinet
el jabón	soap
la toalla	towel
el cortinero, la barra de cortina	curtain rod
el gorro de baño	shower cap
la ducha	shower
la jabonera	soap dish
la esponja	sponge
el champú	shampoo
el desagüe del fregadero	drain

HINT: Keep in mind that depending on the country or the region within a Spanish-speaking country, these vocabulary words might change.

3.8 Superlatives

© TungCheung/Shutterstock.com

The relative superlative describes one noun out of a larger group. For example:

*Rodrigo es el chico **más inteligente** de la clase.* Rodrigo is **the most** intelligent boy in the class.

*Marisol es **la chica más alta** de la clase.* Marisol is **the tallest** in the class.

Other superlatives, such as **peor** or **mejor,** describe the worst/best of a group. For example:

*Este plato es **el mejor** de los tres.* This dish is **the best o**f the three.

*Esta clase es **la peor** de las cuatro.* This class **is the worst** of the four.

Notice that attention must be paid to gender and number when using superlatives.

3.9 The Present Progressive Tense

Verb "to play" – Present Continuous

	affirmative	negative	question
I	I am playing	I am not playing	Am I playing?
he/she/it	He is playing	He is not playing	Is he playing?
you/we/they	You are playing	You are not playing	Are you playing?

Past — NOW — Future

I am doing

© Luna2631/Shutterstock.com

The present progressive tense is used to describe an action that is in the process of happening or an ongoing activity in the present moment. When forming the present progressive, you must use **"to be" (estar)** with the present participle (the second verb).

The present participle is conjugated based on its ending. **-Ar ending** verbs end with **-ando**, while **-er/ir ending** verbs are formed using **-iendo**. For example:

*Yo **estoy estudiando** ahora*. I am studying now.

*Ella **está comiendo** con Ricardo*. She is eating with Ricardo.

*Mi madre **está viviendo** con mi tío*. My mother is living with my uncle.

> **HINT:** There are irregular participles in the present progressive tense. For example:

venir	viniendo
dar	dando
decir	diciendo
oír	oyendo
poder	pudiendo
ser	siendo
traer	trayendo
ver	viendo
construir	construyendo
dormir	durmiendo
pedir	pidiendo

reír	riendo
seguir	siguiendo
sentir	sintiendo
ir	yendo

3.10 Study Tip

© fizkes/Shutterstock.com

Sometimes, you may encounter words in Spanish that look like English words. While most of these might have similar meanings across the two languages, there are some that do not. These are called **false cognates,** or *amigos falsos*. Here are a few examples:

embarazada	means pregnant, not embarrassed
éxito	means success, not exit
molestar	means to be bothered by or annoyed, not molest
constipación	means a cold, not constipation
fábrica	means factory, not fabric
sopa	means soup, not soap

realizar	means to do or perform, not realize
pie	means foot, not pie
ropa	means clothing, not rope
vaso	means glass, not vase

Always be sure to double check the meaning of new words. Find reliable online dictionaries to assist with this.

3.11 Vocabulario: The Dining Room

© Artazum/Shutterstock.com

el vaso	glass
la servilleta	napkin
el cuchillo	knife
el tenedor	fork
la cuchara	spoon
el plato	plate
la porcelana fina	fine china

el chinero, la vitrina	china cabinet
la lámpara de araña	chandelier
la jarra	pitcher
la mesa	table
el pimentero	pepper shaker
el salero	salt shaker

3.12 Indirect Object Pronouns

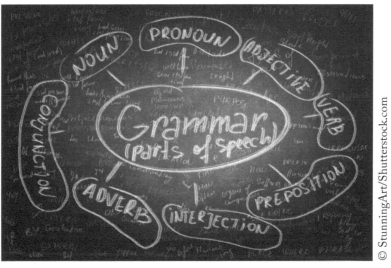

© StunningArt/Shutterstock.com

In Spanish, indirect object pronouns are used to replace nouns or phrases. It tells you for whom or to whom something is being done. Indirect object pronouns in Spanish are:

me	to/ for	me
te	to/for	you
le	to/for	Ud., he, she
nos	to/for	Us
les	to/for	them, Uds.

You previously used indirect object pronouns with **verbs like gustar**. Here is an example, in English, of an indirect object pronoun:

I threw the ball **to him**.

You bought the gift **for her**.

In Spanish:

*Ella **le** compra el regalo.* She buys the gift for her.

*Nosotras **les** compramos la comida.* We buy the food for them.

While the purpose of the indirect object pronouns is the same, the word placement is different. In English, we typically put the indirect object pronoun at the end of the sentence. In Spanish, it is placed (in general) between the subject and the verb. To provide clarification of who the indirect object pronoun refers to, you can do this:

*Ella **le** da la casa **a Marisol**.* She gives the house to Marisol (to her).

*Nosotras **les** damos las toallas **a Erica** y **a Esteban**.* We give the towels to Erica and Esteban (to them).

> **HINT:** You can also place an indirect object pronoun at the end of a verb that hasn't been conjugated. For example:
>
> *Yo voy a darte el regalo.* I am going to give the gift to you.
> *Ella va a darnos los platos.* She is going to give the plates to us.

3.13 Direct Object Pronouns

© Undrey/Shutterstock.com

Direct object pronouns are used to replace a direct object. A direct object is a noun that directly receives the action in the sentence. Because direct object pronouns represent nouns, you must pay attention to both gender and number when using third-person singular and plural ones in Spanish. For example:

me	me
te	you
la	(singular, feminine) it, her
lo	(singular, masculine) it, him
nos	us
los	(plural, masculine) them, Uds
las	(plural, feminine) them, Uds

The word placement is the same as it is for indirect object pronouns.

Yo compro la comida. Yo la compro.	I buy the food. I buy it.
Tú tienes la mesa. Tú la tienes.	You have the house. You have it.

When using indirect object pronouns and direct object pronouns together, the word order is:

Subject + indirect object pronoun + direct object pronoun + verb

*Yo **te** doy el **regalo**. Yo **te lo** doy.* I give you the gift. I give it to you.

*Nosotros **te** damos **los cuchillos**. Nosotros **te los** damos.* We give the knives to you. We give them to you.

> **HINT:** You cannot pair le/les with la/lo/los/las. When you need to do this, you replace le/les with "se." For example:
>
> *Yo **le** doy **los platos**. Yo **se los** doy.* I give him the plates. I give them to him.
> *Nosotros **les** damos **los tenedores**. Nosotros **se los** damos.* We give them the forks. We give them to them.

HINT: While the indirect and direct object pronouns usually appear between the subject and the verb of the sentence, they can also be placed at the end of a sentence when the verb has not been conjugated or when working with the present progressive tense. When adding indirect or direct object pronouns to the present progressive verb forms, put an accent mark on the first vowel after the stem. For example:

Yo quiero vendérselo.
Nosotros estamos mirándola.

3.14 Vocabulario: The Bedroom

© Beyond Time/Shutterstock.com

el despertador, el reloj de alarma	alarm clock
la cama	bed
la almohada	pillow
la cobija, la manta	blanket
la cómoda	chest of drawers
el espejo	mirror
la percha, la suspensión de ropa	clothes hanger

el joyero	jewelry box
el peine	comb
el cepillo	brush

3.15 The Future Tense

© PX Media/Shutterstock.com

The future tense is used to describe future actions just like in English. Remember that the "ir + a" construction expresses future tense connotations; however, it is not the *actual* future tense. To conjugate verbs in the future tense, follow these models:

-ar ending verbs (hablar)

hablaré	I	will speak
hablarás	you	will speak
hablará	he, she, Ud.	will speak
hablaremos	we	will speak
hablarán	you (formal, plural), they	will speak

-er and -ir ending verbs (comer and vivir)

comeré	I	will eat
comerás	you	will eat
comerá	he, she, Ud.	will eat
comeremos	we	will eat
comerán	you (formal, plural), they	will eat
viviré	I	will live
vivirás	you	will live
vivirá	he, she, Ud.	will live
viviremos	we	will live
vivirán	you (formal, plural), they	will live

HINT: As with other tenses in Spanish, there are irregular verbs in the future tense. Here are a few with their stem changes:

decir	dir
haber	habr
hacer	har
poder	podr
ponder	pondr

querer	querr
saber	sabr
salir	saldr
tener	tendr
valer	valdr
venir	vendr

3.16 Vocabulario: The Living Room

© Artazum/Shutterstock.com

el sofá	sofa
la mesa de café, mesa de centro	coffee table
la lámpara	lamp
la mesita	end table
el sillón reclinable	recliner

la escalera	staircase
el techo	ceiling
el muro	wall
la pintura	painting
el jarrón	vase
la chimenea	mantel

3.17 Ordinal Numbers

© fredex/Shutterstock.com

Ordinal numbers are used in Spanish just like they are used in English—to express first, second, third, etc. Here are the ordinal numbers 1-10 in Spanish:

primero	first
segundo	second
tercero	third
cuarto	fourth
quinto	fifth
sexton	sixth

séptimo	seventh
octavo	eighth
noveno	ninth
décimo	tenth

When using **primero** or **tercero** before a masculine noun, drop the "o" off the end, much in the same way as when using "mal" versus "malo." For example:

El primer hombre. The first man.

El tercer día. The third day.

As with other words in Spanish, pay attention to gender and number. For example:

Es el noveno día. It is the ninth day.

La segunda clase del día es muy difícil. The second class of the day is very difficult.

Susana es la primera dentista en el país. Susana is the first dentist in the country.

3.18 Vocabulario: The Kitchen

© Pixel-Shot/Shutterstock.com

el fregadero	sink
la estufa	stove
El refrigerador	refrigerator
el horno	oven
la microonda	microwave
el gabinete	cabinet
el plato escurridor	dish drainer
la vaporizador	steamer
el abrelatas	can opener
la sartén	frying pan
el abrebotellas	bottle opener
el colador	colander
la cacerola, la olla	saucepan
la tapa	lid
el estropajo	scouring pad
la licuadora	blender
la cazuela	casserole dish

3.19 Demonstrative Adjectives

This and That

In Spanish, demonstrative adjectives are used to express or identify the relative position of a noun in time or space. Each demonstrative adjective should agree in gender and number with the noun that it modifies.

When using a version of **este**, keep in mind that whatever noun is being modified is physically close to the speaker.

este/esta	this
estos/estas	these

Any version of **ese**, however, is a bit further away:

ese/esa	that
esos/esas	those

Aquel is used when the object is within sight, but out of reach:

aquel, aquella	that (over there)
aquellos, aquellas	those (over there)

Examples:

Este chico escucha la radio. This boy listens to the radio.

Esta camiseta cuesta demasiado. This shirt costs too much.

Este suéter cuesta menos que ese. This sweater costs less than that one.

Esos muchachos nunca asisten a la clase. Those boys never attend the class.

Esas mujeres son más simpáticas que estas. Those women are nicer than these.

Aquel edificio es más hermoso que ese. That building (over there) is more beautiful than that one.

Aquella camiseta es más interesante que esa. That shirt (over there) is more interesting than that one.

3.20 Un Momento Cultural: Music in Venezuela

© Gil C/Shutterstock.com

Venezuela is famous for specific types of music and dance, primarily the **joropo**, a traditional musical form, and merengue. Merengue is found primarily in larger cities like Caracas.

The joropo is difficult to describe in that it can represent an event, the music performed at the event, or the corresponding dance to the music. The joropo is best characterized by its fast-paced music and its polyrhythmic improvisation. The primary instrument is the plains harp, also known as **arpa llanera**. Clearly the joropo is a part of Venezuelan plains culture the way that the **gaucho** is a part of Argentine frontier culture.

Cited from http://carnaval.com/venezuela/music/

3.21 Un Momento Cultural: Gauchesque Literature in Argentina

Earlier you learned about the gaucho, the Argentine cowboy. In addition to being a major figure in the creation of frontier life on the pampas, the gaucho is also so popular that a literary genre developed around him. This genre is called **la literatura gauchesca**. In many gauchesque works, such as José Hernández's *Martín Fierro* (1872), the gaucho is a symbol of Argentina's past. Because of this, he is oftentimes persecuted by those who believe in modernization and industry. In later works, such as Ricardo Guiraldes's *Don Segundo Sombra* (1926), the gaucho became a symbol of Argentina's future. For this reason, Güiraldes's gaucho characters participate in modernized ranching on the frontier. While the zenith of the gauchesque was between 1880–1920, gauchesque works were still being produced after this time period.

Capítulo 4
PROFESSIONS

50 PROFESSIONS

© YUCALORA/Shutterstock.com

4.1 Estar and Adjectives

You have already learned how to use **estar** to describe current locations, health, or well-being. In contrast to conjugating estar in the present tense, when using estar with adjectives, the adjectives must agree in number and gender with the subject of the sentence. For example:

*Rodrigo está ocupad**o***. Rodrigo is busy.

*Vanessa y María están ocupad**as***. Vanessa and María are busy.

*Él está enferm**o***. He is sick.

4.2 Vocabulario: Adjectives

© Faizal Ramli/Shutterstock.com

The following are adjectives that can be used with ser or estar depending on context. Gender and number must always be considered.

alto	tall, high
bajo	short, low
gordo	fat
flaco	thin
ancho	wide
estrecho	narrow
grande	big
pequeño	small
viejo	old
mayor	older (person)
joven	young

abierto	open
cerrado	closed
antipático	unpleasant
simpático	pleasant, nice
cariñoso	affectionate
estricto	strict
estudioso	studious
generoso	generous
inteligente	intelligent
independiente	independent
feliz	happy
triste	sad
orgulloso	proud
avergonzado	embarrassed
tímido	shy
extrovertido	outgoing
rico	rich
pobre	poor
educado	educated
grosero	rude

bonito	pretty
guapo	goodlooking
feo	ugly
raro	odd
extraño	strange
tacaño	cheap/stingy
precioso	gorgeous
asqueroso	disgusting
bueno	good
malo	bad

El horno está limpio.

Below are common adjectives used with estar (because they express emotions or conditions).

abierto/a	open
aburrido/a	bored

cansado/a	tired
cerrado/a	closed
confundido/a	confused
contento/a	happy
desordenado/a	messy
enamorado/a	in love
enojado/a	angry
limpio/a	clean
listo/a	ready, smart
nervioso/a	nervous
ocupado/a	busy
preocupado/a	worried
sucio/a	dirty
triste	sad

HINT: The past participle can also be used with estar to describe the "ed" or "en" endings in English. For example:

Los niños están perdidos. The children are lost.
La carta está escrita. The letter is written.
El supermercado está cerrado. The supermarket is closed.

Notice the participle must agree in gender and number with estar, the same as with adjectives.

4.3 Impersonal Se

The impersonal se is used to make general observations about what people are doing. The impersonal se is always used with the third-person singular conjugation of a verb. However, the subject of the sentence can be "one," "you," or "they." The subject is never clear which is why this construction is called impersonal. For example:

Se vive mal en esta comunidad. Life is bad in this community.

Se habla español en esta oficina. Spanish is spoken in this office.

Se trabaja mejor con ayuda. You work better with help.

4.4 Passive Se

Like the impersonal se, the passive se is used to talk about actions without referring to who is committing the action. Often this construction is used with direct objects. In contrast to the impersonal se, when using the passive se, the verb must agree with the implied subject. For example:

© Kunst Bilder/Shutterstock.com

Se buscan profesores inteligentes. Intelligent professors are wanted.

Se vende café aquí. Coffee is sold here.

4.5 Tú Commands

© WindAwake/Shutterstock.com

In Spanish, the imperative is used to issue commands (when you want someone to do or not do something). Commands have the same meaning in Spanish as they do in English; however, the verb conjugations of the tú commands are a bit irregular when compared to English command forms. For example:

Affirmative tú commands

Compra la ropa. (You) buy the clothing.

Estudia más. (You) study more.

Lee menos. (You) read less.

> **HINT:** Notice that when working with the tú commands, the verbs are conjugated using the third-person singular form (Ud., él, and ella) instead of the tú conjugation.

Negative tú commands

When telling someone not to do something, use the tú form of the verb. However, reverse the endings, meaning that -ar ending verbs will be conjugated like -er/ir ending verbs, and vice versa. For example:

No compres la ropa. Don't buy the clothing.

No estudies más. Don't study more.

No escribas menos. Don't write less.

4.6 Present Perfect Tense

Present Simple

Present Continuous

Present Perfect

Past Simple

Past Continuous

Past Perfect

Future Simple

Future Continuous

Future Perfect

I have worked

You haven't worked

Have you worked?

Have I worked?

You have worked

I haven't worked

He hasn't worked

Has she worked?

He has worked

© Luna2631/Shutterstock.com

The present perfect tense involves using **haber** (to have), the auxiliary verb, and a main verb. Haber is conjugated like this:

yo	he	I have
tú	has	you have
ella, él, Ud.	ha	she, he, you (formal)
nosotros	hemos	we have
ellos, ellas, Uds.	han	they have

The main verb is conjugated like this:

er and -ir ending verbs	-ido
-ar ending verbs	-ado

For example:

comer	comido
hablar	hablado

As a compound tense, the present perfect means "to have done" something. For example:

Yo he tomado el examen. I have taken the exam.

Ella ha comido la cena. She has eaten the dinner.

Nosotros hemos cantado en el coro. We have sung in the choir.

© Aleksandr Ozerov/Shutterstock.com

Nosotros hemos visto la playa.

4.7 Vocabulario: Health, Beauty, and Ailments

© Alta Oosthuizen/Shutterstock.com

la farmacia	pharmacy/drugstore/chemist
la parafarmacia	herbal pharmacy
la farmacéutica/o	pharmacist
el médico	doctor (male)

el doctor	doctor (male)
la doctora	doctor (female)
el médico de cabecera	family doctor
la enfermera	nurse
el centro de salud	health center/doctor's surgery
urgencias	ER
la salud	health
el hospital	hospital
la ambulancia	ambulance
el practicante	person who would give injections (old fashioned)
la pastilla	tablet
el comprimido	tablet
la píldora	pill
el dolor	pain
me duele	I'm in pain/it hurts
me duele la cabeza	my head hurts
picar	to itch
pinchar	to inject (needle)
la sangre	blood
la consulta	consulting room

la cita previa	(booked) appointment
la receta	prescription
la baja	doctor's note signing you off as sick
el alta	doctor's note signing you fit to work
el hueso roto	broken bone
la vacuna	vaccine
la droga	drug
el medicamiento	medication
la medicina	medicine
la dosis	dosage
estar embarazada	to be pregnant
respirar	to breathe

Other expressions

alta presión sanguínea	high blood pressure
el dolor de cabeza	headache
el dolor de estómago	stomachache
el dolor de garganta	sore throat
el dolor	ache

4.8 Vocabulario: Clothing

© Creative Lab/Shutterstock.com

el albornoz	bathrobe
el cinturón (leather belt, cinturón de cuero)	belt
la blusa	blouse
las botas	boots
los bóxers	boxers
el sostén, el sujetador, el brasier	bra
la gorra, el gorro	cap
el abrigo	coat
el vestido	dress
los guantes	gloves
el traje, el vestido, el vestido de noche, el vestido de baile (formal dress)	gown
halter, top	halter

el sombrero (any kind of hat)	jacket hat
la chaqueta	
los jeans, los vaqueros, los bluyines, los tejanos	jeans
las mallas (can refer to any type of tight-fitting elastic clothing)	leggings
los leggings	leggings
la minifalda	miniskirt
la pijama	pajamas
los pantalones	pants, trousers
el bolsillo	pocket
el bolso	purse
el impermeable	raincoat
la sandalia	sandal
la camisa	shirt
el zapato	shoe
cordones, agujetas (primarily in Mexico)	shoelaces, shoestrings
los pantalones cortos, el short, las bermudas, el culote (especially cycling shorts)	shorts
la falda	skirt
la zapatilla	slipper
el calcetín	sock

la media	stocking
el traje	suit
el suéter, el jersey, la chompa	sweater
la sudadera, el pulóver (with hood, con capucha)	sweatshirt
el traje de entrenamiento (literally, training clothes)	sweatsuit
el bañador, el traje de baño	swimsuit
el zapato de tenis, el zapato de lona	tennis shoe, sneaker
la corbata	tie
top (women's clothing article)	top
la camiseta, la playera	T-shirt
el esmoquin, el smoking	tuxedo
la ropa interior	underwear
el reloj, el reloj de pulsera	watch, wristwatch

HINT: The most common verbs associated with clothing are: llevar, ponerse, and tener.

4.9 Vocabulario: Professions

© VAKS-Stock Agency/Shutterstock.com

contador, contable	accountant
actor/actriz	actor/actress
administrador	administrator
embajador, embajadora	ambassador
arqueólogo	archaeologist
arquitecto	architect
artista	artist
atleta	athlete
abogado	attorney
panadero	baker
barbero	barber
mesero	bartender
esteticista	beautician
biólogo	biologist
hombre/mujer de negocios, empresario	businessman/businesswoman
carnicero	butcher
capitán	captain
carpintero	carpenter
farmacéutico	chemist (pharmacist)

químico	chemist (scientist)
director general	chief executive officer
oficinista	clerk (office worker)
dependiente	clerk (retail worker)
entrenador	coach
programador	computer programmer
cocinero	cook
bailarín/ bailarina	dancer
dentista	dentist
médico	doctor, physician
conductor	driver
redactor	editor
electricista	electrician
ingeniero	engineer
agricultor, granjero	farmer
bombero	firefighter
florista	florist
geólogo	geologist
guardia	guard
hotelero	hotelier, innkeeper

joyero	jeweler
cronista	journalist
rey/reina	king/queen
dueño	landlord
bibliotecario	librarian
cartero	mail carrier
mecánico	mechanic
comadrona	midwife
ministro	minister (politics)
pastor	minister (church)
modelo (no separate feminine form)	model
músico	musician
enfermero	nurse
optómetra	optometrist
pintor	painter
piloto (separate feminine form rarely used)	pilot
poeta	poet
presidente/presidenta	president
profesor, catedrático	professor

sicológico	psychologist
rabino	rabbi
marinero	sailor
dependiente, vendedor	salesman/saleswoman
científico	scientist
secretario	secretary
criado	servant
asistente social	social worker
soldado	soldier
estudiante	student
cirujano	surgeon
maestro, profesor	teacher
terapeuta	therapist
veterinario	veterinarian
camarero, mesero	waiter
soldador	welder
escritor	writer

4.10 Negative Words in Spanish

EPS 10

© serenaarts/Shutterstock.com

You have already learned how to negate a verb's action by placing "no" in front of it. There are other words of negation in Spanish, namely:

nadie	nobody
nada	nothing
ni	nor
ni...ni	neither...nor
jamás	never
nunca	never

tampoco	neither, not either
todavía no	not yet
ya no	no longer

When using these words, you are permitted (as mentioned in a previous chapter) to use double or even triple negatives. For example:

No hay nadie en la clase. There is no one in the class.

No hay esperanza nunca. There is never hope.

Notice with the English translations, there is only one negative word, rather than two. You can also use these words instead of "no." For example:

Nunca camina aquí. He never walks here.

Nadie nada aquí. No one swims here.

When using **ningún, ningunas, ninguna,** pay attention to the gender of the noun that is being negated. For example:

No tengo ningún libro. I don't have a book.

No tienes ninguna amiga. You don't have a friend.

Only use ninguno when you are using it without a noun afterward. For example:

Tengo algún libro. I have some book.

No hay ninguno. There are none.

There are also affirmative words in Spanish. For example:

algo	something
alguien	someone
alguno/a/as	a, one, any, some

siempre	always
alguna vez	ever
también	also
o ... o	either ... or

Yo leo siempre las novelas. I always read the novels.

Tú conoces a Celia Cruz también. You also know Celia Cruz.

4.11 Using Commands to Give Advice

© fizkes/Shutterstock.com

You have already learned how to give affirmative and negative informal commands. Now you will learn how to use commands for giving advice. For example:

For a student who needs help in class, you could say: *estudia más*

For a friend who smokes, you could say: *no fumes*

Notice that when giving advice in an informal situation, you use the tú command conjugation forms.

4.12 Study Tips

© Jacob Lund/Shutterstock.com

Remembering vocabulary can be difficult. Start with words that look like words in English, such as *literatura* (literature) and *biología* (biology). Always verify the meanings of the words first to make sure that they mean what they look like. From there, keep a notebook or use an app on your phone to keep track of words that you use on a regular basis, but that you don't know in Spanish. By focusing on words that you use the most, you will build vocabulary in a way that is most helpful to you.

Capítulo 5
ADDRESSING DIFFERENT GROUPS OF PEOPLE

El pelícano nada por el mar.

5.1 Por and Para

In Spanish, many of the prepositions most commonly used have multiple meanings. However, like other grammatical concepts in Spanish, the context determines which one to use. Two prepositions that work like this are **por** and **para**.

Por:

- The most commonly used context for por is when it means by or through. The context is used to demonstrate travel or communication. For example:

María camina por el parque. María walks through the park.

Yo viajo a la casa de mis parientes por autobús. I travel to the house of my relatives by bus.

- Por also means "for" in the sense of a specific duration of time. For example:

Tú trabajas por ocho horas cada día. You work for eight hours each day.

Yo leo por cuatro horas. I read for four hours.

- Por is also used for financial exchanges. The English translation would be "for." For example:

Yo compro la computadora por sesenta dólares. I buy the computer for 70 dollars.

Ella compra la blusa por siete dólares. She buys the blouse for 7 dollars.

- When talking about the reasons for doing something, you will use por.

Para:

- Para is used to describe destinations. Many times, you will see para associated with the future tense in this context. For example:

Mi madre sale para Ecuador. My mother leaves for Ecuador.

Ellos salen para España mañana. They leave for Spain tomorrow.

- Para is also used for deadlines, again associating it with the future tense. For example:

Necesita estudiar las materias para este viernes. She needs to study the subjects by this Friday.

Tengo que completar la presentación para las ocho. I have to finish the presentation by eight.

- If someone is the recipient of a gift, then you use para. For example:

Tengo un regalo para Esteban. I have a gift for Esteban.

Mis padres compran un regalo para mí. My parents buy a gift for me.

- If you have a goal, such as becoming a part of a specific profession, then you would use para. For example:

Yo trabajo para ser médico. I work to be a doctor.

Mi hermana quiere ser abogada. My sister wants to be a lawyer.

5.2 Expressions Using Por and Para

© PattaraSiri/Shutterstock.com

por los pelos	barely	por lo menos	at least
día por día	day by day	por lo mismo	for that very reason
estar por	to be in the mood to	por lo que a mí me toca	as far as I'm concerned
palabra por palabra	word for word	por lo que he oído	judging by what I've heard

por adelantado	in advance	por lo tanto	therefore
por ahí, allí	around there	por lo visto	apparently
por ahora	for now	por malo que sea	however bad it is
por amor de Dios	for the love of God	por medio de	by means of
por aquí	this way	por mi parte	for my part
por casualidad	by chance	por motivo de	on account of
por ciento	percent	por ningún lado	nowhere
por cierto	certainly	por orden	in order

por completo	completely	por otra parte	on the other hand
por correo	by mail / post	por poco	almost
por dentro	inside	por primera / última vez	for the first / last time
por desgracia	unfortunately	¿por qué?	why / for what reason
por Dios	oh my God / for heaven's sake	por separado	separately
por ejemplo	for example	por si acaso	just in case
por escrito	in writing	por su propio mano	by one's own hand
por eso	therefore / that's why	por suerte	fortunately
por favor	please	por supuesto	of course
por fin	finally	por teléfono	on the phone, by phone
por la mañana	in the morning	por la tarde	in the afternoon
por la noche	in the evening	por todas partes	everywhere
por las buenas o por las malas	whether you like it or not	por todos lados	on all sides / everywhere
por lo común	usually	por último	Finally
por lo demás	furthermore	por una parte	on the one hand
por lo general	generally / in general	por un lado, por otro	on one hand, on the other hand

estar para	to be about to
para abajo	down, downward
para adelante	forward
para detrás	backward
para entonces	by that time
para esa época	by that time
para otra vez	for another occasion
para que	so that, in order that
para qué	why for what purpose
para siempre	forever
para variar	just for a change
ser tal para cual	to be two of a kind

5.3 Formal Commands

Formal commands (Ud. and Uds.) work in a similar way as informal commands (tú). When working with Ud. formal commands, you conjugate the verbs by reversing the endings, meaning that -ar ending verbs use the -er/ir verb endings and vice versa. Uds. commands follow the same rule using the plural form. These types of command forms are used in formal situations, such as speaking with your employer or a professor.

© antoniodiaz/Shutterstock.com

For example:

Ud. singular formal command form

Ud.	coma
Ud.	viva
Ud.	escriba
Ud.	tome

Uds. plural command form

Uds.	coman
Uds.	vivan
Uds.	escriban
Uds.	tomen

There are many irregular verbs in Spanish, even when using formal commands. Here's a list of common irregular verbs in their Ud./Uds. command forms.

tener	tenga/an
hacer	haga/an
poner	ponga/an
poder	pueda/an
traducir	traduzca/an
traer	traiga/an
jugar	juegue/en

decir	diga/an
pedir	pida/an
dormir	duerma/an

5.4 Time Expressions with Hacer

In Spanish, you use **hacer** to describe how long you have been doing something. Just follow this structure:

Hace + (amount of time) + que

Hace dos años que hablo italiano. I have been speaking Italian for two years.

Hace quince años que manejan. They have been driving for fifteen years.

You can also use **desde hace** + time to indicate the same thing. For example:

No estudié gramática desde hace veinte años. I have not studied grammar for twenty years.

Tú no corres desde hace dos meses. You have not run for two months.

5.5 Vocabulario: Shopping

© Rawpixel.com/Shutterstock.com

el super	supermarket (short form)
el carro	trolley
la cesta	basket
el parking	car park
el aparcamiento	car park
¿algo más?	anything else?
la panadería	bakery
la carnicería	butcher
el pasillo	aisle
los congelados	frozen foods
la comida fresca	fresh food
la cola	queue
la caja	cash register
la dependienta	shop assistant

la hora de apertura	opening times
el mostrador	display counter
el reponedor	packer
el frutero	grocer
la frutería	fruit and vegetables section
la báscula	weight scale
el descuento	discount
la oferta	offer
la bolsa	bag
el cajero/la cajera	checkout assistant
el vigilante de seguridad	security guard

5.6 More with Formal Commands

© Roman Samborskyi/Shutterstock.com

When do you use formal commands? It all depends on your relationships with other people. While some people might have an informal relationship with their employer, other people may not. If you are unsure whether to use informal tú commands or formal Ud./Uds. commands, then always err on the side of caution and use the formal command form. Here are a few additional examples to help you navigate formal commands.

Sea interesante. Be interesting.

Abra la puerta. Open the door.

Abra las ventanas. Open the windows.

Estudie más. Study more.

Aprenda una lengua extranjera. Learn a foreign language.

Coma más verduras. Eat more vegetables.

Lea más. Read more.

As you can see from these examples, many commands function as advice (telling someone how to improve his/her health, etc.). Whether you are using tú or Ud./Uds. commands, you can think of these forms as offering or giving advice to another person or persons.

5.7 Past Perfect Tense

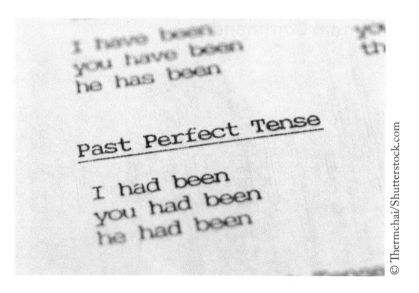

© Thermchai/Shutterstock.com

The past perfect tense is used to describe what you "had done" before something else happened in the past. It also requires haber like the present perfect tense. However, you use the imperfect conjugation of haber. For example:

yo	había	I had
tú	habías	you (informal) had
ella, él, Ud.	había	she, he, you (formal) had
nosotros/as	habíamos	we had
ellos, ellas, Uds.	habían	they, you (formal, plural) had

After forming haber, you use the past participle endings: -ido for -er/ie ending verbs and -ado for -ar ending verbs. For example:

Yo había corrido por la calle cuando ellos llegaron. You had run through the street when they arrived.

Esteban y Marco habían hablado en francés cuando sonó el teléfono. Esteban and Marco had spoken in French when the phone rang.

Ella no había estudiado antes de ahora. She had not studied before now.

5.8 Vocabulario: Restaurant

© Soleskz/Shutterstock.com

| la mesera, la camarera, el mesero, el camarero | waitress/waiter |
| el cocinero | cook |

la mesa	table
la cuenta	check
el menú	menu
el/la ayudante de camarero	busboy
un recibo	receipt
el plato principal	main dish
el aperitivo	appetizer
un postre	dessert
soda/ refresco	soda
el café	coffee
el vino tinto	red wine
el vino blanco	white wine
el pan, el panecillo	dinner roll
la cuchillería	cutlery
el cuchillo	knife
el tenedor	fork
la cuchara	spoon
un cuchillo de carne	steak knife
la servilleta	napkin

5.9 Hace to Mean "Ago"

We have already looked at hace + time + que to describe a certain period of time. Using hace + a period of time with the preterite tense means "ago." For example:

Estudié fotografía hace dos años. I studied photography two years ago.

Leyó la novela, The Great Gatsby, *hace seis meses.* She read the novel, *The Great Gatsby,* six months ago.

Fuimos a la playa hace un mes. We went to the beach a month ago.

5.10 Using Object Pronouns with Commands

When object pronouns with positive commands, attach them to the end of the conjugated verb. For example:

Escriba la carta. Escríbala. Write the letter. Write it.

Traiga la tarea. Tráigala. Bring the homework. Bring it.

> **HINT:** Add an accent to verbs with two or more syllables or to verbs that have one or more object pronouns like in the examples above. If a verb has one syllable, only add an accent when there are double object pronouns.

When using double object pronouns with commands, place the indirect object pronoun first followed by the direct object pronoun. For example:

Háztelo. Do it.

Cómamelos. Eat them for me.

> **ADDITIONAL HINT:** Remember that third-person singular and plural direct object and indirect object pronouns cannot be together. Replace the indirect object pronoun (le or les) with se.

When using negative commands, you cannot attach object pronouns to the end of the verb. Instead, you must place them between the "no" and the conjugated verb. Indirect object pronouns appear first, followed by direct object pronouns. For example:

No le dé el anillo. No se lo dé. Don't give the ring to her. Don't give it to her.

No me visites. Don't visit me.

5.11 Irregular Commands with Tú

© fizkes/Shutterstock.com

When using the tú command form, you will come across irregular verb forms. The most common are:

decir	di
poner	pon
hacer	haz
ir	ve
salir	sal
ser	sé
tener	ten
venir	ven

5.12 Nosotros Commands

When working with nosotros commands, the Spanish meaning is the English equivalent of "let's." It is used with a group of people. For example:

Contemos las cartas. Let's count the cards.

Hablemos con amigos. Let's speak with friends.

Leamos las revistas. Let's read the magazines.

> **HINT:** When working with a positive command using "ir," it will look like this:

Vamos temprano. Let's leave early.

When working with a negative command, it will look like this:

No vayamos con ellos. Let's not go with them.

When attaching double object pronouns to the end of a nosotros command, make sure to remove the "s" from the nosotros form when working with "se." For example:

Escribámosela. Let's write it for them.

This same command form can be created using the ir + a construction. For example:

Vamos a ir al bosque. Let's go to the forest.

Vamos a cruzar la calle. Let's cross the street.

Vamos a leer la novela. Let's read the novel.

To negate the command, just put "no" in front of the verb. For example:

No nademos aquí. Let's not swim here.

No leamos este libro. Let's not read this book.

When working with objects with negative commands, place the object between the "no" and the verb form. For example:

No lo escribamos. Let's not write it.

No lo leamos. Let's not read it.

Reflexive verbs and nosotros commands: When working with reflexive verbs, include them in your nosotros commands. For example:

No nos lavemos. Let's not wash ourselves.

Vamos a lavarnos. Let's wash ourselves.

Lavémonos. Let's wash ourselves.

5.13 Un Momento Cultural: Accents in Spain

© Eszter Szadeczky-Kardoss/Shutterstock.com

The accent in Spain is very distinct. It is often referred to as the "Spanish lisp." You can form this accent by converting a "c" into a "th" sound. For example: cero—pronounced as *the-ro* or canción—pronounced *can-the-own*.

No other Spanish-speaking country uses the Spanish lisp. Native Spaniards will use the "th" sound when pronouncing a "z" or a "c" followed by an "i" or an "e."

5.14 Study Tips

You have probably been told that memorization is not useful when learning a foreign language. Really, it depends on what you are trying to memorize. If you are absently trying to remember random words, you probably won't remember them beyond a test or a quiz. There are useful tips that can help you, though.

The best way to avoid wasting time memorizing is to pay attention to patterns. When thinking about irregular verbs in the present tense like dormir or poder, for example, recognize that the same verbs are often irregular in other tenses. While this won't help you remember the verb endings for every tense, it will alert you to the fact that there is a pattern with these verbs outside of their endings. In addition to this, there are certain syllables that require an accent mark, or another pattern in Spanish. For example, canción or televisión. Whenever you have a "ción" or "sión" ending in a noun, you will have an accent mark. Again, this won't help you remember vocabulary words like televisión, but it will help you remember another crucial detail when working with nouns: accent marks.

Capítulo 6
THE WORLD

© PopTika/Shutterstock.com

6.1 Infinitive Commands

We have looked at informal, formal, and nosotros commands. An infinitive verb (one that hasn't been conjugated) can also be used to issue commands. For example:

*No **mezclar** los ingredientes.* Don't mix the ingredients.

*No **fumar** en la oficina.* Don't smoke in the office.

***Comer** más fruta.* Eat more fruit.

Infinitive commands can be helpful if you find yourself having trouble remembering other command forms. These commands can be used in informal and formal settings.

6.2 Relative Pronouns

Relative pronouns are words that refer back to previously mentioned nouns.

Relative pronouns can be used to tie two distinct sentences together. For example, when using **que** (who, whom, that, and which):

Yo compré un libro ayer. I bought a book yesterday.

El libro es muy complejo. The book is very complex.

Yo compré un libro que es muy complejo. I bought a book that is very complex.

> **HINT:** Notice that que is related to the most important noun in the sentence: libro.

In this content, que means: that, which, who, or whom.

Quien/quienes is another relative pronoun that is typically used with people. It means who or whom. For example:

Ricardo, quien es médico, es el primo de Rodrigo. Ricardo, who is a doctor, is Rodrigo's cousin.

Mi amiga, quien vive en Nueva York, va a ir a Perú este fin de semana. My friend, who lives in New York, is going to go to Peru this weekend.

If you use quien/quienes in the direct object position of the sentence, you can use quien/quienes or que. It must agree in number with the antecedent. For example:

La señora que conocí en la fiesta es la amiga de Esteban. The woman whom I met at the party is Esteban's friend.

If quien/quienes is used directly with people, then you have to include the personal "a." For example:

La señora a quien conocí en la fiesta es la amiga de Esteban.

El que, la que, los que, and **los que** are also relative pronouns. They typically translate into English as "the one" or "the ones," depending on whether they are modifying singular or plural nouns. Notice that when using these relative pronouns, you must pay attention to gender in addition to singular versus plural. For example:

*Mi **primo**, **lo que** es estudiante, va a graduarse en diciembre.* My cousin, the one who is a student, is going to graduate in December.

*Mis **primas**, **las que** son escritoras, están escribiendo una novela.* My cousins, the ones who are writers, are writing a novel.

6.3 Relative Adjectives

© TungCheung/Shutterstock.com

Relative adjectives relate to that which is owned. The closest translation in English is "whose." As with lo que, la que, etc., pay attention to gender and number when using cuyo, cuya, cuyos, and cuyas. For example:

*El gato, **cuyo dueño** vive aquí, es muy amistoso.* The cat, whose owner lives here, is very friendly.

*La estudiante, **cuyo padre** dirige la escuela, quiere estudiar arte.* The student, whose father leads the school, wants to study art.

6.4 Future Perfect Tense

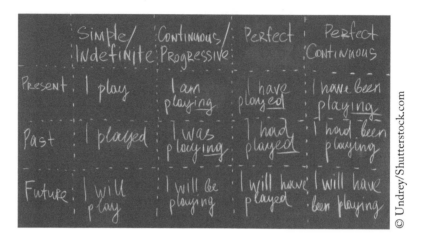

© Undrey/Shutterstock.com

The future perfect tense is used to describe what will have happened by a specific time or after a different action takes place in the future. Start by using haber:

yo	habré
tú	habrás
él, ella, Ud.	habrá
nosotros/as	habremos
ellos, ellas, Uds.	habrán

The past participle remains the same as in the present perfect tense. For -ar ending verbs, it will be -ado and for -er/ir ending verbs, it will be -ido. There are always irregular participles like escribir (escrito) and abrir (abierto). For example:

Habré escrito la carta para la mañana. I will have written the letter by the morning.

Habremos salido para esta noche. We will leave by tonight.

Cuando Esteban salga, nosotros habremos llegado al restaurante. When Esteban leaves, we will have arrived at the restaurant.

6.5 Sino Versus Pero

In Spanish, **sino** means but rather and **pero** means but. While their meanings are slightly similar, they are used in different ways. Sino is used when the second part of the sentence contradicts the first, whereas pero is used when this is not the case. For example:

Yo necesito ir al supermercado, pero no tengo tiempo. I need to go to the supermarket, but I do not have time.

Marco es un buen estudiante, pero es antipático. Marco is a good student, but he is unpleasant.

Nosotros tenemos un gato, pero queremos un perro. We have a cat, but we want a dog.

Tú no compras fresas, sino queso. You do not did not buy strawberries, but rather cheese.

No me acuesto tarde, sino temprano. I don't go to bed late, but rather early.

Ella no va al gimnasio, sino a la biblioteca. She does not go to the gym, but rather the library.

6.6 Other Prepositions

Prepositions and examples taken from: https://www.livingspanish.com/Preposiciones-I.htm

ante and **antes:** before, against, about

- *Están ante mí* They are before me.

- *Ante mi respuesta todos quieren argumentar* Before my answer, everyone wants to argue.

bajo: beneath, under

- *El perro está bajo la silla* The dog is beneath the chair.

cabe (junto): together, alongside, near

- *Escucho junto a la puerta* I listen near the door.

con: with

- *Trabajo con Miguel* I work with Miguel.

desde: from; since, for

- *Desde ayer no has comido* You have not eaten since yesterday.

durante: during

- *Quieres ir al parque durante el descanso* You want to go to the park during the break.

en: in or on

- *En el horno está el pollo asado* The roast chicken is in the oven.

- *Prefiero viajar en autobús* I prefer to travel on the bus.

entre: between; among

- *Estaban entre la escuela y la biblioteca* They were between the school and the library.

- *La blusa estaba entre la ropa limpia* The blouse was among the clean clothes.

hacia: towards

- *Hacia la izquierda y verás la calle* Towards the left and you will see the street.

hasta: until, up till, usually in relation to time

- *Hasta hoy no tengo que trabajar* I did not have to work until today.

- *Te esperaré hasta las tres* I will wait for you until three.

según: according to

- *Según Antonio, no necesitamos estudiar* According to Antonio, we do not need to study.

sin: without

- *Me gusta la ropa sin adorno* I like clothing without adornment.

excepto y salvo: an exception or but

- *Estaban todos allí, excepto mi tío, Julio* They were all there except for my uncle Julio.

- *Todos los estudiantes estaban allí salvo los nuevos graduados* All the students were there except the new graduates.

sobre: on, about, indicates place or approximate time

- *Sobre las cinco voy a cenar* I am going to have dinner about five.

- *Sobre la mesa está el mantel* The tablecloth is on the table.

tras: after, following, behind, indicates time and place

- *Tras la ventana escuchemos toda la conversación* We listen to the whole conversation behind the window.

6.7 Vocabulario: Countries and Cities

© Cvijovic Zarko/Shutterstock.com

Alemania	Germany
Antártida	Antarctica
Austria	Austria
Bélgica	Belgium
Brasil	Brazil
Bulgaria	Bulgaria
Canadá	Canada
Chipre	Cyprus
Dinamarca	Denmark
Escocia	Scotland
Eslovaquia	Slovakia
Eslovenia	Slovenia
España	Spain
Francia	France
Gales	Wales
Grecia	Greece
Hungría	Hungary
Inglaterra	England
Irlanda	Ireland
Islandia	Iceland

Luxemburgo	Luxembourg
Marruecos	Morocco
Nueva Zelanda	New Zealand
Países Bajos	Netherlands
Polonia	Poland
Rumanía	Romania
Reino Unido	United Kingdom
Los Estados Unidos	United States
Sudáfrica	South Africa
Suecia	Sweden
Suiza	Switzerland

6.8 Vocabulario: Animals

el elefante	elephant
el león	lion
el hipopótamo	hippopotamus
el rinoceronte	rhinoceros
el cuerno	antler
la trompa	trunk
el colmillo	tusk
el tigre	tiger
el alce	moose
el oso	bear
la llama	llama
la cebra	zebra
el bisonte	bison
el caballo	horse
el burro	donkey
la oveja	sheep
el venado	deer
el chivo	goat
la jirafa	giraffe
el cerdo	hog
la vaca	cow

6.9 Un Momento Cultural: Urban Places in Spain

© kavalenkau/Shutterstock.com

In Spanish cities like Madrid, residents are used to taking the metro subway system from the city center, all throughout the city, as well as to surrounding neighborhoods. As a result, Madrid residents walk more often than most inhabitants in American cities. One can live fairly comfortably without a car in Madrid. At the same time, neighborhoods are walkable, meaning necessary shops and stores are close to where residents live. This decreases the amount of driving they need to do. It even decreases the amount of time that residents take the subway.

Other differences in city living include customs like the siesta. During the majority of the afternoon, shops and stores close to observe the siesta. At the time, most residents go home to have lunch, the biggest meal of the day. Spaniards relax at home and spend time with their families before returning to work. For this reason, dinner, one of the smallest meals of the day, is held at nine or ten o'clock in the evening.

In most city centers like Madrid, one can find green spaces like El Parque del Buen Retiro. Within the parks, people rent canoes, walk, or lounge beneath the many trees that provide shade. Parks like this one provide residents with a green space that contrasts with the typical developments seen in larger cities.

6.10 Study Tips

Reading in Spanish

Reading in Spanish can seem intimidating; however, it is the best way to build vocabulary and be exposed to grammatically correct sentences. Start by reading smaller passages or stories, like fairy tales. Fairy tales utilize basic vocabulary and simple storylines. When these become easier, increase the level of difficulty of the reading passage. You could try to read online newspaper articles about your favorite things such as sports or movies. Even with passages like these, you will be exposed to specialized vocabulary associated with the subject matter. As your confidence builds, try reading short stories, excerpts from novels, or even novels themselves. While you may not know every single word, you will know many of them. The more that you expose yourself to reading in Spanish, the more vocabulary you will learn.

Capítulo 7
ENTERTAINMENT

7.1 Conditional Tense

The conditional tense is used to express probability, so it is often associated with the English translations "would," "could," "must have," or "probably." Use the conditional tense:

1. To express ideas about the past

2. To express the future from the perspective of the past

3. To express actions that may or may not happen

125

4. To be polite in situations like ordering in a restaurant

5. To express actions that can't occur because of another action

6. To ask advice

7. To express what might happen in a certain situation

For example:

Me gustaría tomar un vaso de agua. I would like to have a glass of water.

El profesor necesitaría calificar más. The professor should grade more.

Nosotros estaríamos en casa. We must have been at home.

Regardless of whether the verbs are -ar, -er, or -ir ending, they follow the same conjugation rules. To conjugate verbs in the conditional tense, follow this model:

yo	estaría
tú	estarías
ella, él, Ud.	estaría
nosotros/as	estaríamos
ellos, ellas, Uds.	estarían

7.2 Irregular Verbs in the Conditional Tense

© Lamai Prasitsuwan/Shutterstock.com

As with the other tenses in Spanish, there are irregular verbs in the conditional tense. Here is a list of common verbs that are irregular in the conditional tense:

caber	yo cabría
poner	yo pondría
decir	yo diría
haber	yo habría
salir	yo saldría
hacer	yo haría
poder	yo podría
tener	yo tendría
querer	yo querría
valer	yo valdría
saber	yo sabría
venir	yo vendría

Notice that most of the irregular verbs listed here tend to be the same verbs that are irregular in other tenses like the present, the present subjunctive, to name a few.

7.3 Past Anterior Tense

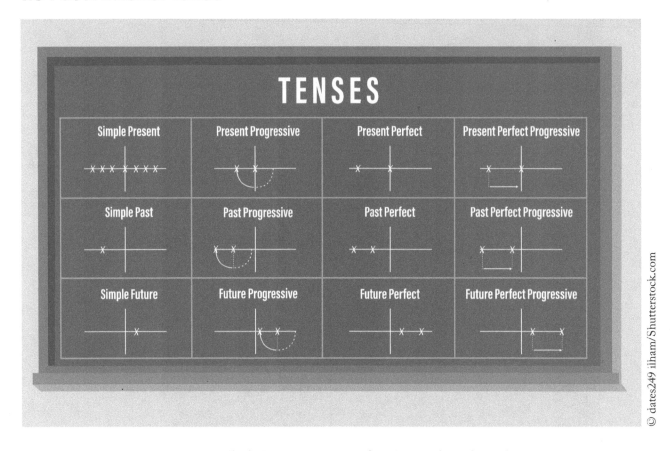

© dates249 iiham/Shutterstock.com

The past anterior tense, also called the preterite perfect, is used to describe a past action that happened before another past action. This tense is rarely used in spoken Spanish. Rather, it is found in formal writing. Despite the fact that it is not used very often in spoken Spanish, it is still important to learn so that you can navigate different writing forms in Spanish.

Conjugating the verbs in this tense requires using the preterite tense form of haber, along with the past participle that is used in the present perfect, etc. The past participle is formed like this: -ar ending verbs become -ado (hablado) and -er/ir ending verbs become -ido (asistido). For example:

yo	hube hablado
tú	hubiste hablado
ella, él, Ud.	hubo hablado
nosotros/as	hubimos hablado
ellos, ellas, Uds.	hubieron hablado

It can be translated as "had spoken."

Other examples:

Hubo terminado cuando ella empezó a llorar. I had finished when she began to cry.

Hubimos comido cuando nosotros miramos la televisión. We had eaten when we watched television.

7.4 Con and Contra

© GagoDesign/Shutterstock.com

Con and contra are two basic prepositions in Spanish. Con means "with," while contra means "against." Because of the similarity in their spelling, they can be mixed up easily. The context of the sentence always determines which one to use. For example:

Yo trabajo con Ricardo. I work with Ricardo.

Los profesores trabajaron con Juan el semestre pasado. The professors worked with Juan last semester.

Tú luchas contra la opresión. You fight against oppression.

Nosotros trabajamos contra la falta de los derechos de las mujeres. We work against the lack of women's rights.

7.5 Vocabulario: Sports

© Rocksweeper/Shutterstock.com

gym	el gimnasio
warm up	el calentamiento
to stretch	estirar
to be a member	ser socio
locker rooms	los vestuarios
locker	la taquilla
machines	las máquinas
weights	las pesas
to run	correr

to walk	andar
to swim	nadar
to play	jugar
tennis	tennis
football	fútbol
badminton	el bádminton
squash	el squash
rugby	el rugby
horse riding	la equitación
scuba diving	el buceo
sailing	la vela
paddleball	el pádel
golf	el golf
gymnastics	la gimnasia
racing	carreras
basketball	el baloncesto
cricket	el críquet
watersports	los deportes acuáticos
cycling	el ciclismo
martial arts	los artes marciales

to fish	pescar
hockey	el hockey
to ski	esquiar
volleyball	el vóleibol
to skate	patinar
baseball	béisbol
boxing	boxeo
lacrosse	el lacrosse
goooooooooooaaaaal	goooooooooooool
the rules	las normas
goalkeeper	el portero
referee	el árbitro
triathlon	el triatlón
marathon	el maratón
golf clubs	los palos de golf
racket	la raqueta
ball	la pelota
ball	la bola
ball	el balón

7.6 Un Momento Cultural: The Frontier

© lu_sea/Shutterstock.com

Las obras de Jorge Luis Borges

Jorge Luis Borges was an Argentine writer (1899–1986) most famous for his short stories that bridged several different literary genres, primarily the *gauchesque* and magical realism. His short story, "El Sur" (The South) describes the imagined adventures of a library secretary, Juan Dahlmann. Bored by his life as a simple office worker expected to complete the same tasks over and over again, Dahlmann begins to dream of an entirely different world after contracting blood poisoning. The story is often classified as either a part of "lo fantástico," or magical realism because it combines elements of reality as we know it (the humdrum world of work and the expectation of living a stable, predictable life) with an imagined frontier. At the end of the story, the reader is left wondering whether or not Dahlmann's knife fight with gauchos is real or imagined.

The ambiguity in Borges's works illustrates the very questions that he attempted to answer during his writing career: what is reality? How does reality form us and then, unexpectedly, disappoint us? Why do we turn to imagined recreations of the past to give us solace in the present moment? These questions, illustrated through Borges's simple or overly complex plots, bring to light our quest for understanding our identity and how we are formed by the society around us.

Additional Resources

Jorge Luis Borges
https://www.britannica.com/biography/Jorge-Luis-Borges

Argentine Writers
https://lithub.com/beyond-borges-5-argentine-writers-you-should-know/

7.7 Un Momento Cultural: Argentine Film

© gnepphoto/Shutterstock.com

El cine argentino

Despite the fact that many silent films are still available to watch in the United States, in Argentina, this is not always the case. One of the few remaining films from 1915, *La Nobleza gaucha* (Gaucho Nobility), manages to give us an idea of Argentine culture at the beginning of the twentieth century.

La Nobleza gaucha describes the adventures of Juan, a gaucho on the frontier, who journeys to Buenos Aires in order to save his girlfriend, María, from the clutches of a wealthy landowner, Don Gran. Don Gran has spent years brutalizing his gaucho employees on the frontier while indulging in drink in Buenos Aires. At the end of the thirty-minute film, Juan saves María and returns to the frontier safely with her.

At the time of its production, many social issues such as xenophobia and concerns about class conflict proliferated across Argentina. Eduardo Martínez de la Pera illustrates these concerns by championing the purity of a different time: the gaucho and frontier life. While wealthy landowners like Don Gran abuse their power and class status, Juan always remains true to his sense of ethics garnered from his life on the Argentine frontier.

Looking at silent films from Argentina gives us the opportunity to see both the similarities and the differences between Argentine and American concerns at the beginning of the twentieth century. Like many Americans, Argentines turned to the past, viewing it as a simpler, more manageable time period than the industrial world of the early twentieth century. Yet, the frontier, for both Americans and Argentines was riddled with conflict, disease, and a struggle to survive, a contrast from how it is depicted in the cultural imagination. Watching older films like *La Nobleza gaucha* allows us to see how Argentines viewed themselves and the world around them during changing times.

Additional Resources

Argentine Film
https://www.latinolife.co.uk/node/257

Argentine Cinema
https://www.oxfordbibliographies.com/view/document/obo-9780199791286/obo-9780199791286-0246.xml

7.8 Un Momento Cultural: Mexican Literature

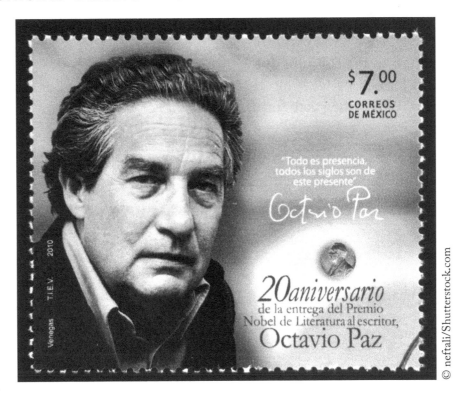

$7.00
CORREOS DE MÉXICO

"Todo es presencia, todos los siglos son de este presente"

Octavio Paz

20aniversario
de la entrega del Premio
Nobel de Literatura al escritor,
Octavio Paz

Venegas   T.I.E.V.   2010

© neftali/Shutterstock.com

La literatura mexicana: Juan Rulfo

Like Julio Luis Borges, Juan Rulfo dabbled in different writing styles and genres to explore his quest for understanding humanity. In contrast to Borges, Rulfo's work is extremely specific in theme. Many of his texts, such as *Pedro Páramo*, attempt to understand the abuse of power as it works internally. In *Pedro Páramo*, for example, Juan Preciado journeys to his mother's hometown in order to find his father, the infamous Pedro Páramo. In a twist reminiscent of Borges's "El Sur," Preciado finds more than he bargained for when he ends up unknowingly joining Comala's dead. Because Páramo has abused the town that he is supposed to care for as its *cacique*, the town's inhabitants eventually succumb to his abuses, dying off one by one.

Clearly, a criticism of Mexico's *caciquismo*, a Carib term that means to "clean house," Rulfo permits Comala's most marginalized inhabitants to voice their stories as they tell Preciado about their past. Like Borges's work, Rulfo incorporates elements of the fantastic when he creates major characters that are already deceased from the novel's opening pages.

Additional resources

Mexican Literature: History and Political Climate of Mexico
http://thelatinoauthor.com/countries/literature/mexican-literature/

Juan Rulfo
https://www.britannica.com/biography/Juan-Rulfo

7.9 Present Subjunctive Tense

A Brief Introduction to the Subjunctive

The subjunctive is formed by reversing the endings to the verbs. So -ar ending verbs like hablar will take on -er/ir ending verb forms like comer. For example:

Estudiar – to study

yo	estudie
tú	estudies
ella, él, Ud.	estudie
nosotros/as	estudiemos
ellos, ellas, Uds.	estudien

Comer – to eat

yo	coma
tú	comas
ella, él, Ud.	coma
nosotros/as	comamos
ellos, ellas, Uds.	coman

CAPÍTULO 7: Entertainment

The present subjunctive is used to talk about wishes, emotions, doubt, disbelief, denial, recommendations, nonexistent or intangible things. In English, the present tense would be used; however, in Spanish, the present subjunctive must be used in situations like these. For example:

Wishes

Yo quiero que tú estudies más. I wish that you would study more.

Emotions

Es triste que los hombres no encuentren trabajo. It is sad that the men cannot find work.

Doubt and disbelief

No creo que tú seas la presidenta del club. I do not believe that you are the president of the club.

Recommendations

Yo recomiendo que las chicas salgan más con amigas. I recommend that the girls go out more with friends.

Nonexistent or intangible things

Necesito a alguien que pueda entender el proceso. I need someone who can understand the process.

7.10 Study Tips

Working with tenses in Spanish that are very different from their English counterparts can make learning Spanish difficult. The best way to deal with tenses like the present subjunctive or reflexive verbs in Spanish is to understand the verb forms first. Try to come up with tricks for remembering the verb endings as well as any irregular verb forms in that tense.

Once you can remember the verb forms, look at the uses of the tense. You might want to stick with literal translations of the sentences so that the verb uses make more sense to you. Literal translations can make the verb use more apparent than accurate translations. Then, once you feel comfortable, try to use more accurate translations. These tips can help you navigate tenses that do not have exact translations in English.

© Anton Violin/Shutterstock.com

8.1 The Present Perfect Tense

Present Simple

Present Continuous

Present Perfect

Past Simple

Past Continuous

Past Perfect

Future Simple

Future Continuous

Future Perfect

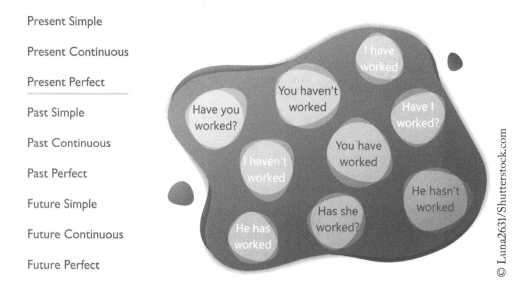

© Luna2631/Shutterstock.com

The present perfect tense, also called the *pretérito perfecto compuesto* or *el antepresente*, is used to talk about what has happened in the recent past. These actions are repeated or continue in some form in the present tense. The present perfect is used in a similar way in English. For example:

Yo he hablado. I have spoken.

Tú has escrito. You have written.

To form the present perfect, you have to use the verb **haber (to have)** along with the past participle of another verb. First, let's look at how to conjugate **haber** in the present perfect:

yo	he
tú	has
ella, él, Ud.	ha
nosotros/as	hemos
ellos, ellas, Uds.	han

To form the participle of regular verbs, follow this formula:

-er/ir	-ido ending
-ar	-ado ending

For example:

bailar	bailado	danced
comer	comido	eaten
vivir	vivido	lived

Typically, the ending in English would be **-ed** or **-en**.

For example:

I have writt**en**.

I have spok**en**.

I have visit**ed**.

Irregular participles:

hacer	hecho
ir	ido
escribir	escrito
decir	dicho
volver	vuelto
ver	visto
abrir	abierto

As always, with irregular verbs, you have to memorize them.

8.2 The Past Perfect Tense

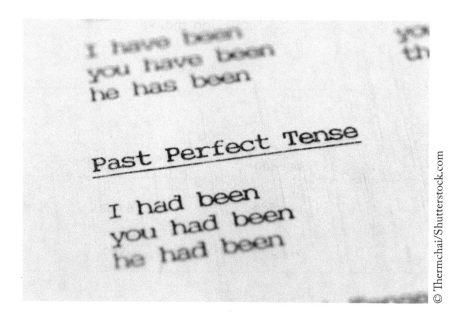

© Thermchai/Shutterstock.com

The past perfect tense or the *pretérito pluscuamperfecto* or *el antecopretérito*, is used to talk about a past action that occurs before another past action. Like the present perfect, it requires the verb **haber (to have)** and a past participle.

Haber is formed in the past perfect like this:

yo	había
tú	habías
ella, él, Ud.	había
nosotros/as	habíamos
ellos, ellas, Uds.	habían

The past participle is formed the same way as it is in the present perfect:

-ado ending
-ido ending

hablado

comido

vivido

The irregular participles are the same as they are in the present perfect tense.

You will typically see the past perfect used alongside the basic past tenses in Spanish, such as the preterite. For example:

Yo había hecho las maletas cuando llegaste. I had packed the bags when you arrived.

Ella había salido antes de cenar. She had left before having dinner.

Nosotros habíamos comido cuando el teléfono sonó. We had eaten when the phone rang.

8.3 The Future Perfect Tense

Verb "to go" - Future Perfect

7

	affirmative	negative	question
I	I will have gone	I won't have gone	Will I have gone?
he/she/it	He will have gone	He won't have gone	Will he have gone?
you/we/they	You will have gone	You won't have gone	Will you have gone?

© Luna2631/Shutterstock.com

The future perfect tense, also called *el futuro compuesto*, is used to talk about something that will have happened or will have been completed at some point in the future. Like the present and past perfect tenses, it uses **haber (to have)**.

Haber is formed like this:

yo	habré
tú	habrás
ella, él, Ud.	habrá
nosotros/as	habremos
ellos, ellas, Uds.	habrán

The future perfect tense also uses the past participle. Like the present and past perfect tenses, the past participle is formed like this:

-ar	-ado ending
-er/ir	-ido ending
hablar	hablado
comer	comido
vivir	vivido

Here are some examples of the future perfect tense and its meanings:

Yo habré terminado mi tarea esta noche. I will have finished my homework by tonight.

Tú habrás comido la cena cuando yo llegue. You will have eaten when I arrive.

8.4 The Future Tense

© patpitchaya/Shutterstock.com

The simple future tense, or *el futuro simple*, is used to talk about what will or shall happen in the future. You can form the future tense like this:

yo	hablaré
tú	hablarás
ella, él, Ud.	hablará
nosotros/as	hablaremos
ellos, ellas, Uds.	hablarán

Examples:

Yo hablaré con el profesor mañana. I will speak with the professor tomorrow.

Nosotros hablaremos con nuestros abuelos este fin de semana. We will speak with our grandparents this weekend.

The endings for the simple future tense are the same for -ar, -er, and -ir ending verbs.

You can also describe the future using the **ir + a construction**. This is often referred to as the informal future. For example:

Yo voy a hablar con el profesor mañana. I am going to speak with the professor tomorrow

Tú vas a hablar con tus abuelos este fin de semana. You are going to speak with your grandparents this weekend.

8.5 Vocabulario: Money

© ElenaR/Shutterstock.com

un descubierto	an overdraft
El cajero automático	ATM, cash machine
una deuda	a debt
recaudar fondos	raise funds
acciones	shares

pagar	pay
una cuenta bancaria	a bank account
la tarjeta de crédito	credit card
el saldo	bank balance
la herencia	inheritance
un descuento	a discount
la caja, caja registradora till,	cash register
el dinero en efectivo	cash
un billete	a banknote
la alcancia /hucha	money box, piggy bank
una cartera	a wallet
una hipoteca	a mortgage
una moneda	coin
invertir	invest
un recibo	a receipt
la bolsa	the stock market
tener suficiente dinero para comprar algo	to afford

8.6 Vocabulario: Financial

© Hand Robot/Shutterstock.com

acer un ingreso	to deposit
retirar dinero	to withdraw money
el banco	the bank
abrir una cuenta	to open an account
cancelar una cuenta	to close an account
la oficina bancaria	bank office
la sucursal bancaria	bank branch
el número de la cuenta	banking account
la cuenta de ahorro	savings account
el titular de la cuenta	account holder

8.7 Un Momento Cultural: Parks in Latin America

© Mikolaj Niemczewski/Shutterstock.com

Tayrona National Park, Colombia

Set along Colombia's Caribbean Coast, about an hour-long drive from the boho-beach town of Santa Marta, is one of the most incredible national parks in South America. With an untouched coastline and miles of jungle flora and fauna, Tayrona is an ideal off-the-grid retreat with plenty to keep active types busy. Hike to spot wildlife like red howler monkeys, capuchin monkeys, cotton-top tamarin, iguanas, dart frogs, and more. Go snorkeling to uncover the area's coral reefs; or just relax on the pristine beaches.

Iguazu National Park, Argentina and Brazil

The breathtaking falls sit on the Brazil-Argentina border and span across almost two miles with national parks in both countries. There are various trails and ways to experience the cascades: the famous Devil's Throat, one of the "new seven wonders of the world," is located on the Argentina side and accessed by an open-air jungle train; the Brazilian side is perfect for hikers, with a relatively easy 40-minute hike to the falls.

Sajama National Park, Bolivia

For adrenaline seekers and outdoor lovers, Sajama National Park is home to Bolivia's snowy volcanoes (the highest peak being Navajo Sajama), hot springs, geysers, plenty of llamas and alpacas, and a welcoming indigenous population found throughout the Aymaran communities. Visit this Andean landscape during the dry season from April to November; traveling with a tour operator is recommended.

Los Roques National Park, Venezuela

Hundreds of acres of coral reefs, white-sand beaches, and warm waters make this national park the largest marine park in the Caribbean Sea. The 300-plus islands and cays are located about 80 miles from Venezuela's capital, Caracas, and attract visitors for kite surfing, diving, and sport fishing.

All info written here taken from: https://www.jetsetter.com/magazine/10-incredible-national-parks-in-south-america-to-add-to-your-bucket-list/

8.8 Study Tips

Is memorization a bad idea when learning languages? In some ways, yes. For example, if you are trying to memorize random vocabulary words without a context or entire passages just to complete an exam, then you are not making the most of your time. However, if you are memorizing numbers, verb tense forms, or irregular verbs, then this is all a part of the process for learning another language. Over time, you should be able to rely less on memorization and more on intuition. In other words, the verb forms that you used to have to memorize will now be a part of your working vocabulary and knowledge base. As a result, you will "know" these forms without having to look them up.

How do you do this? First, memorize a few verbs at a time. Then start using them. Put them in a context that you would utilize on a regular basis. The more that you use the verb forms that you are memorizing, the more that you will understand them so that notecards or other memorization techniques will not be necessary.

Capítulo 9
THE OUTDOORS

9.1 The Conditional Tense Review

© Rob Wilson/Shutterstock.com

The conditional tense in Spanish is used to make polite requests, like in a restaurant, or to talk about hypothetical situations. It is also called *el condicional* and *el pospretérito*.

To form the conditional tense, you add the same endings for -ar, -er, and -ir ending verbs like this:

yo	comería	I would like to eat
tú	comerías	you (informal) would like to eat
ella, él, Ud.	comería	he/she/you (formal) would like to eat
nosotros/as	comeríamos	we would like to eat
ellos, ellas, Uds.	comerían	they/you all would like to eat

There are a few irregular verbs in this tense:

| tener | tendría |
| poner | pondría |

valer	valdría
salir	saldría
venir	vendría
haber	habría
querer	querría
saber	sabría
decir	diría
hacer	haría

Here are some examples of the uses of the conditional tense:

Me gustaría tomar un café. I would like to have a coffee.

Nosotros tendríamos un apartamento nuevo. We would have a new apartment.

9.2 The Present Subjunctive Review

As already discussed, the present subjunctive tense is used to express wishes, emotions, impersonal expressions, recommendations, and doubt/denial.

The present subjunctive is formed using opposite endings. -ar ending verbs take on -er/ir endings and vice versa. For example:

hablar	yo hable
comer	yo coma
escribir	yo escriba

Hablar

yo	hable
tú	hables
ella, él, Ud.	hable
nosotros/as	hablemos
ellos, ellas, Uds.	hablen

Escribir

yo	escriba
tú	escribas
ella, él, Ud.	escriba
nosotros/as	escribamos
ellos, ellas, Uds.	escriban

There are many irregular verbs in the present subjunctive. To know which ones are irregular, think of the "yo" form in the present tense. Is it irregular? If so, then you will use this stem and then add the subjunctive endings. For example:

tener	yo tengo (present tense)	yo tenga (present subjunctive)
salir	yo salgo (present tense)	yo salga (present subjunctive)

Other irregular verbs:

traer	traig
querer	quier
poner	pong
hacer	hag
decir	dig
conocer	conozc
poder	pued
saber	sep
haber	hay
ir	vay
dormir	duer
pedir	pid

Below is an example of expressing a **wish or a want** using the present subjunctive:

Yo espero que tú estudies más. I hope that you study more.

Notice that in English, we use the present tense for the entire sentence, whereas in Spanish, after the que, you use the present subjunctive. Before the que, you use the present tense.

Below are examples of a recommendation, impersonal expression, emotion, and doubt/denial.

Yo recomiendo que ella estudie más. I recommend that she studies more.

Es necesario que tu niño aprenda otro idioma. It is necessary that your child learn another language.

Me alegro que ellos se casen. I'm glad that they are getting married.

Dudo que ella escriba una novela en español. I doubt that she writes a novel in Spanish.

9.3 The Imperfect Subjunctive Tense

© Yury Zap/Shutterstock.com

Imperfect Subjunctive

The imperfect subjunctive, or the *imperfecto subjuntivo*, is usually associated with "si clauses" ("if" clauses) to describe something unlikely or impossible. What differentiates the imperfect subjunctive from the present subjunctive is not the conditions that trigger this tense, but rather the past tense context used to describe these events (usually in conjunction with the preterite or the imperfect), the conditional, or the past perfect.

To form the imperfect subjunctive, you conjugate the verbs like this:

Tener (-er ending)

yo	tuviera
tú	tuvieras
ella, él, Ud.	tuviera
nosotros/as	tuviéramos
ellos, ellas, Uds.	tuvieran

Escribir (-ir ending)

yo	escribiera
tú	escribieras
ella, él, Ud.	escribiera
nosotros/as	escribiéramos
ellos, ellas, Uds.	escribieran

Tocar (-ar ending)

yo	tocara
tú	tocaras
ella, él, Ud.	tocara
nosotros/as	tocáramos
ellos, ellas, Uds.	tocaran

There are a few irregular verbs with stem changes:

decir	dij
ir	fuer
hacer	hic
pener	tuv
poder	pud
poner	pus
querer	quis
saber	sup
ser	fuer
sentir	sint
ver	vier
leer	ley

Examples of the uses:

Yo quería que tú hablaras español. I wanted you to speak Spanish.

Era bueno que tú estuvieras todos los días. It was good that you studied every day.

Si tuviera más dinero, viajaría. If I had more money, I would travel.

Si mi madre tuviera más dinero, volvería a la universidad. If my mother had more money, she would return to the university.

Quisiera tres semanas de vacaciones. I would like three weeks of vacation.

Esperaba que mi hermana se casara. I hoped that my sister was getting married.

9.4 Vocabulario: The Outdoors

© Yevhenii Chulovskyi/Shutterstock.com

la mochila	backpack
la playa	the beach
la bicicleta	the bicycle
la bic	the bike
la fogata	the bonfire
la pesca	fishing
la caminata	the hike
la caza	the hunt
el bicho	the bug
el bosque	the forest
las botas	the boots

la botella	the bottle
el campamento	the camp
la canoa	the canoe
el disco volador	frisbee
la hamaca	the hammock
la hoguera	the campfire
el mapa	the map
la leña	the firewood
la mesa de picnic	picnic table
el lago	lake
el paseo	walk
el saco de dormir	sleeping bag
la salchicha	hot dog
la tienda de campaña	tent
el malvavisco	marshmallow
la linterna	flashlight
la cerilla	the match

9.5 Un Momento Cultural: Outdoor Activities

© Mike Pellinni/Shutterstock.com

https://www.inspirock.com/outdoor-venezuela

South America has many natural sites that are famous for everything from waterfalls to wildlife. Below are a few of them:

Laguna de la Restinga, Margarita Island

The Laguna de la Restinga is known for its indigenous wildlife. You can see pelicans, starfish and jellyfish because of the clear water, and mangrove forests. In many respects, it resembles parts of Florida and the Caribbean.

Angel Falls in Venezuela

The water cascades nearly 979 m (3,211 ft), with 807 m (2,647 ft) of free-falling water. Located in Canaima National Park, the falls are tucked away in a remote area of the park, reached by a long hike.

Mt. Roraima, Canaima National Park

This particular mountaintop resembles a tabletop. It is located between Guyana, Brazil, and Venezuela. It is known for having some of the oldest geological formations. It has 1330 ft. cliffs on all sides.

9.6 Study Tips

© mangpor2004/Shutterstock.com

As already mentioned in previous chapters, learning how to speak another language can be very difficult. This is because there are so many processes involved in language use from forming muscles in your mouth to mentally processing information. To form the muscles in your mouth when pronouncing certain words, you need to keep practicing. You can practice speaking even if you don't have a partner or know someone who is a native speaker. Here is how you can find additional opportunities for speaking out loud:

1. Read short passages out loud. This can be from fairytales, your textbooks, online newspapers, and even chat room conversations. Start with words that you know before moving on to words that are unfamiliar. Remember that Spanish is a phonetic language, meaning that each letter is pronounced in a word.

2. Watch Spanish TV shows or podcasts. Repeat the words that you hear. Don't worry if you don't understand everything. Focus on what you *do* understand.

3. Take advantage of free resources like DuoLingo. You can repeat anything that you hear in these apps. The more that you practice, the more that you will build the muscles in your mouth.

4. Be patient. Learning a language, especially the spoken aspect of it, takes time. If you keep practicing, you will get better each time even if you don't think that you are.